4.00

WINDWARD OF

By the same author

THE WALK OF THE OYSTERS

# Windward of the Law

Rex Mackey

Free from all restraint and awe
Just to the windward of the law

CHARLES CHURCHILL,
*The Ghost*

THE ROUND HALL PRESS • DUBLIN

© Rex Mackey, 1965, 1991
First edition, 1965
Second edition, 1991
Reprinted 1992

A catalogue record of this book
is available from the British Library

ISBN 0-947686-76-2
ISBN 0-947686-94-0 pbk

Printed in Ireland
by Colour Books Ltd, Dublin

# Contents

*To Carmel, Noemi and Thora*

# Prologue

The young gentleman approached me with a diffident courtesy that immediately stamped him as either a confidence trickster or an Englishman.

"Do you mind if I speak to you, sir, about something rather important to me?"

"It is traditional from time immemorial for everyone in a Dublin hostelry to speak without formality to everyone else," I replied sententiously. "This pleasant custom, however, does not entail a corresponding obligation of listening."

"I have already observed that but I hope you will make an exception. I should very much like you to join me and perhaps discuss one or two matters which are troubling me."

It transpired that my young friend was indeed an Englishman, in his first term as an undergraduate of Dublin University, more usually known as Trinity. He now wished to be enrolled as a student of the King's Inns with a view to being called to the Irish Bar. Could I help him?

I pointed out the superior advantages of a career as a bookmaker, Irish politician or some such lucrative avocation; but my attempts to dissuade him were unavailing.

I accordingly agreed to help him in his improvident determination.

At this he expressed what I thought a disproportionate

gratitude. He had heard, he said, of giants of learning, eloquence and wit from Curran and O'Connell to Carson and Healy, and he wanted me to tell him more about a profession in such a great tradition.

"As to that," I observed, "even the latest of these luminaries was somewhat before my time, which spans but a fleeting quarter of a century."
"At least you can tell me something about it."
I invited him to be a little more specific.
"Well," he insisted, "something of its history, personalities, judges, cases, and so on—you know the sort of thing I mean. . . ."

Its very enormity stunned me into committing myself to an attempt to comply with this further request. Having done so, however, I can only hope that the following pages will partly satisfy my demanding, but fortunately elastic, terms of reference.

# 1

# In the Beginning

The aspirant to the ancient and noble profession of Barrister-at-Law in Ireland must first have himself enrolled as a student of the King's Inns in Dublin. This simple statement does not, however, begin to describe the obstacles which in the years immediately before the Second World War beset the path of the eager youth. Not the least of these was the personality of the then Under-Treasurer.

This functionary who was, or should have been, the repository of such information necessary to the taking of this step, was distinguished by the infirmities of near blindness, deafness and an impenetrable stupidity. He had also survived to an incredible age and appeared to suffer from the delusion that he was living in Victorian times. This was understandable, because as far as is known he had never emerged into the light of day for the best part of fifty years, other than periodically to cross the courtyard to the Inns' Library, a distance of some fifty yards.

It must be appreciated that the course of legal education at the King's Inns is pursued in conjunction with that of the universities at Trinity and University College, theoretically at any rate. One would have thought, therefore, that some pretence of amity would have been professed between these institutions and the seat of legal learning. This was not the case and an implacable war, so cold as to exclude even the exchange of insulting notes, was maintained between the Universities and the Inns.

The state of affairs was largely because the Under-Treasurer never acknowledged the existence of the other two august bodies, except with reluctance and under duress, an attitude which was reciprocated. The result for the unfortunate undergraduate can be compared to the difficulties in which a blind man would find himself were he parachuted into the middle of the maze at Hampton Court. His only hope lay in enlisting the assistance of some young barrister, called recently enough to remember the toils in which he had struggled. Then, armed with the appropriate documents, he could present Josie with *faits accomplis* and await his signatures. These were often obtained only by refusing to leave the office until he got them.

When, exhausted and dazed from the fray, he was graciously permitted by the Honourable Benchers to be enrolled, he found that it was all worth while.

The trials and tribulations of the neophyte in joining are in the historical tradition of the Inns themselves. Their written history dates back as far as the reign of Edward the First, and ever since they have reflected the turbulence of eight hundred years.

In those early days the Anglo-Norman city of Dublin, comprising a few acres and consisting mainly of the Castle and the two Cathedrals, was surrounded by a wall. Beyond this area the job of serving the King's writ was not one which a life insurance company would view with any great enthusiasm. Even in the immediate environs suburban life was certainly less dull than it later became.

In the fourteenth century the Superior Courts and the lawyers resided at Collet's Inn outside the walls on ground where, roughly speaking, the modern Central Hotel stands, within a stone-throw of Dublin Castle. In 1348 when the Courts were sitting the fierce O'Byrnes, Princes of Wicklow, decided to pay a call. From the fastness of their glens and mountains they descended upon the learned gentlemen of the long robe, who did not wait even to adjourn their cases before precipitately retiring within the Castle walls. They also left behind them the money chests of the Exchequer, a gesture which their visitors greatly appreciated. While the procedure has latterly been altered, this is the first recorded precedent for the formality of taking out the monies lodged in Court. In the reasonable belief that a similar generosity was unlikely to be extended to them for some time to come, the O'Byrnes then proceeded to demolish what was left of Collet's Inn which was not portable.

We do not know very much about how the Judges and lawyers housed themselves for the next few years, except that having retired to the safety of Dublin Castle, they did not feel disposed to emerge again. They were reinforced in this prudent resolution by the invasion of the Bruces which, coming so soon after the contempt of court of the Wicklow men, must have provoked frequent sighs for England, Home and Beauty.

In the circumstances it is not surprising to learn that after the invasion the King sent over his Serjeant-at-Law, one Simon Fitzrichard, at a fee of five marks per annum to re-organize the legal administration of the Pale. His labours must have been to some purpose for in the next reign, that of Edward III, we find that Sir Robert Preston, Chief Baron of the Exchequer, gave up his residence in the city to the legal body, and so the Inns of Court were re-established under the name of Preston's Inn, the Benchers of which admitted counsellors to the practice of the law in Ireland.

This state of affairs continued until 1542 when, on the dissolution of the monasteries, Henry VIII caused the existing Inn and its property to be restored to the Preston family. In the same year he granted to the professors of the law the immensely wealthy "monastery or house of the Friars Preacher near Dublin, and the site, circuit, ambit, and precinct of the said monastery and church with the steeple and cemetery of the same together with all the messuages, edifices, mills, orchards, gardens, lands, tenements, and other hereditaments whatsoever, with the appurtenances of the said monastery or house." This desirable property, situate on the north side of the Liffey, was henceforth known as the King's Inns.

If King Hal was under the impression that the provision of such wealth, amenities, and pleasances, in the fair City of Dublin would create at the Irish Bar that atmosphere of cloistered contemplation so conducive to the peaceful practice of the law which characterized the Inns of Court in London, the events of the next hundred and fifty years were to prove him sadly mistaken. The Bar itself can hardly be blamed, because it can be truly said that throughout this period Ireland was in a continuous state of turmoil, rebellion, and war. This involved the Judges and lawyers, not least because at the beginning of the seventeenth century James I extended to Ireland the circuit system, and sent out the first Justices of Assize.

These attempts to administer English Justice to an unwilling people, who themselves had the Brehon system of immeasurably greater antiquity, were, of course, more of the nature of military expeditions than legal visitations. The result was that dexterity with the sword and pistol was at least as important an educational asset to the Irish barrister, as a knowledge of Bracton or the profundities of Littleton, as recently interpreted by Lord Chief Justice Coke. Thereby was established a tradition at the Bar which survived well into the nineteenth century.

The man chosen by the wisest fool in Christendom for the establishment of the new circuits, was Sir John Davis whose career had discovered personal qualities eminently befitting him for this adventurous undertaking. He had been called to the Bar by the Benchers of the Middle Temple, which Honourable Society shortly disbarred him for conduct which was considered outrageous for even a practising barrister in those days. According to Fosse's *Judges of England*, "on the evening of the 9th February 1597, he came into the dining hall of the Middle Temple with his hat on his head and accompanied by two attendants armed with swords. He then went up to the barristers' table, where a gentleman named Richard Martin was dining, pulled from under his gown a cudgel, which the vulgar call 'a bastinado', and struck him upon the head repeatedly, and with so much violence that the bastinado was shivered into divers pieces. Then returning to the bottom of the hall he drew one of the attendants' swords, and flourished it over his head, turning his face towards Martin, and then turning away adown the water-steps of the Temple, threw himself into a boat." For this behaviour he was "disbarred, expelled the house, and deprived of his authority ever to speak or consult the law."

Sir John, however, was a man not merely of action but of resource, so that in the year of the accession of James Stuart we find him successfully petitioning the Honourable Society for re-admission. His Majesty of Scotland and England, whose influence in this reinstatement one is inclined to suspect, clearly felt that Sir John's talents were peculiarly suited for his Irish kingdom. He sent him to Dublin as his Solicitor-General, soon to be promoted to Attorney-General, and charged with the duties of creating and putting into effect the procedure of sending Judges into the country on Circuit. This entailed largely the mustering of sufficient numbers of cavalry and musketeers to ensure that their Lordships could preside over the Assize Courts without being torn to pieces by a native population, which was so stiff-necked and ungrateful as to refuse to recognize the beneficence of an enlightened code of justice which gave legal sanction to the expropriation of five-sixths of its land and property.

Sir John displayed such a tenacity and devotion to his master's cause in Ireland as to excite honourable feelings of obligation in that notoriously unmindful monarch. For his Irish services he was rewarded with the Lord Chief Justiceship of England. Regrettably he did not live to adorn this great office; one feels he could have set a headline for even

13

such distinguished successors as my Lords Jeffries and Ellenborough.

His Majesty's Judges of the Superior Courts in Ireland from now on set forth from the King's Inns on their precarious Assizes, held twice yearly until the outbreak of the Great Rebellion in 1641. This cataclysm together with the interregnum of Oliver Cromwell who had even less use for lawyers than for politicians, put an effective period to their activities for twenty years. On his Restoration in 1660, however, one of the first acts of Charles II was the appointment of Judges to the Irish Courts. Among them were Sir Jerome Alexander, to the Bench of the Common Pleas, and Sir William Aston, to that of the King's Bench, thereby earning for these two gentlemen a special niche in Irish legal history. It was, improbably, because of a typical piece of carelessness on the part of the Merry Monarch in their appointment, that there grew up a code which was to become an integral part of the mores not only of the Bar, but of Irish society in general. Even more improbably was this practice in the case of the grievances of Alexander and Aston accorded by their colleagues on the Irish bench, a kind of unholy benediction, with far-reaching results.

Properly to understand how this state of affairs came about it is necessary to emphasize that even to this day the members of the Bench and Bar are, if possible, more jealous in the assertion of their privileges *vis-à-vis* each other, than in collectively protecting them against the rest of the world. Without having this professional punctilio before his mind it would appear that Charles II's letter for the appointment of Sir William bore an earlier date than that for Sir Jerome, although their patents passed on the same day and both were sworn together.

Now Sir Jerome was of longer standing in the English Inns, and so he politely published his signed view that he took precedence over his brother judge. This provoked a defamatory, and indeed scurrilous reply, which, although anonymous, left no doubt as to its authorship.

Sir Jerome immediately enlisted the good offices of Patrick D'Arcy, an eminent member of the profession, a scion of one of the original fourteen tribes of Galway, and a gentleman whose hand and services were ever ready in the cause of honour. D'Arcy was instructed to demand an explanation from Aston, who refused to give any or make the slightest concession, whereupon a regular challenge followed.

Despite the fact that Sir William had been a Cromwellian colonel, he discreetly declined the invitation and went so far as to lay a criminal information, not against Sir Jerome but against D'Arcy. The application came before Aston's brethren in the King's Bench, Chief Justice Barry and Mr. Justice Stockton, who peremptorily refused it on the somewhat sophistical grounds that Sir William did not deny in his affidavit that he wrote the libel and was privy to publishing it.

Seldom has a successful litigant heard a judgement with more approval than Patrick D'Arcy Esq., Counsellor-at-Law, who immediately announced to all and sundry that he proposed to horsewhip his lordship Mr. Justice Aston at the first available opportunity, on or off the bench. This ex parte proceeding never took place in fact, not through any fault of D'Arcy's but because Sir William continuing upon his set course of discretion, disappeared from the bench and Irish society for eight years until he heard of D'Arcy's death. He then emerged from his judicious retirement when he was assured that no other learned champion awaited his reappearance to chastise him.

As Oliver Burke, Q.C., tells us in his memoirs "This singular event operated like a patent of indemnity for duels." He never said a truer word, and as we shall see later in greater detail, right into the last century no member of the King's Inns, be he Judge, Bencher or Barrister, would be considered to have begun to be properly qualified unless the conventional inquiry about him "Has he blazed?" could be answered in the affirmative.

The legal situation created by the Restoration had only

15

thirty years to run. In 1691 the Glorious Revolution was treacherously consummated by the dishonoured Treaty of Limerick. A sycophantic Parliament proceeded immediately to enact the infamous Penal Laws which ushered in a century of tyranny and oppression of which the bench and bar in Ireland were the most effective instruments. This appalling code was described by Doctor Johnson as "more grevious than all the ten persecutions of the Christians", and denounced by Edmund Burke as "an infernal code, a machine of wise and deliberate contrivance as well fitted for the oppression, impoverishment, and degradation of a people, and the debasement in them of human nature itself as ever proceeded from the perverted ingenuity of man."

One of these laws provided that no one could sit in the Irish legislature, nor hold any Irish office, civil, military, or ecclesiastical, nor practise law or medicine in Ireland until he had taken the oath of allegiance and supremacy (which declared the King head of the church, and the sacrifice of the Mass damnable), and subscribed to the declaration against transubstantiation. No Catholic judge or barrister could take this oath under pain of excommunication. The vast majority of them were, accordingly, excluded from the administration and practice of the Law, and the ancient Irish, and Anglo-Irish aristocracy and gentry, by reason of their twofold allegiance to their religion and the principle of legitimacy, were deprived even of such meagre and reluctant protection as it still preserved.

As a result the Irish judiciary and bar was composed of men who owed their privilges to either treason or apostacy, or both. On the bar messes on Assizes, or at other convivial legal occasions throughout the eighteenth century, were drunk toasts of such devoted loyalty to the Hanoverian monarchy as would have deepened the already rubicund hue of the royal countenance had he understood the English language.

While protesting their allegiance to the teutonic House of Guelph, however, it is right to say that they were not unmindful of the fountain and origin of their present fortunes. It was customary therefore to conclude the post-prandial demonstrations with a toast to William of Orange in the following terms:

Here's to the pious, and immortal memory of King Billy, who saved us from knaves and knavery, slaves and slavery, Popes and popery, brass money and wooden shoes. And if any man among us refuse to rise to this toast, may he be slammed, crammed and jammed into the barrel of the great gun of Athlone. And may the gun be fired into the Pope's belly, and the Pope into the Devil's belly, and the Devil into the roasting pit of Hell, and may the door of Hell be banged shut and the key kept in the pocket of a brave Orange boy. And may there never lack a good Protestant to beat hell out of a Papish. And here's a fart for the Bishop of Cork.

History does not inform us how the reverend incumbent of that historic See had offended the pious susceptibilities of the heirs of the Glorious Revolution. We do know, however, that they were further exacerbated in 1793. In that year George III was bullied into signing the Catholic Relief Act which did such violence to his conscience as to cause him to relapse into insanity. As a result of this enactment some of the more opprobrious disabilities under the Penal Laws were removed.

Catholics could now practise at the Bar (although not until 1829 could they become Judges or K.C.s) on swearing an oath of allegiance which did not offend against their religious beliefs. In effect, 1796 was the first year in which they could be called on the completion of their legal education; from then on they were admitted in ever increasing numbers. By a curious coincidence 1796 was also the year in which the Four Courts were ready for the reception of the Judges. It was on Monday November 8 1796 that the Superior courts first sat in the building which, except for a brief interval, they have occupied ever since.

This permanence of residence on the North bank of the Liffey was a pleasant change for their lordships who, hitherto, might have been described as of no fixed abode. Before this time, for example, the seat of justice had been situated on

17

the other side of the river near Dublin Castle in a part of Christ Church Cathedral yard. This building was, as it were, the focal point of a perfect warren of side streets and alleyways where the more dubious characters of the town, not excluding the bar, were in the habit of resorting. The taverns most commonly patronized by the practitioners were to be found in an area known as Hell, and strangers inquiring for some learned counsel were not infrequently startled when advised to "Go to Hell and look for him." On reflection, they might have concluded that it was not such an unlikely place in which to find a lawyer.

The new building was designed by the great James Gandon whose design was submitted to the Lord Chancellor and Chief Judges and approved by them with orders to proceed in 1785. His son, James, in his admirably succinct notes describes the work:

The Four Courts were built on ground formerly occupied by the King's Inns.

Excavations began 1st October 1785, but owing to various obstructions were not ready until the 3rd March 1786 when His Grace the Duke of Rutland, accompanied by the Lord Chancellor and Chief Judges, in state, laid the first stone.

Originally a grant of £3,000 per annum was given for the construction, later increased to £6,000 and in all a grant of £60,234 was made.

It was not until 1798 that the foundations were laid for the East wing of the remaining offices, nor, owing to the political events, was it until 1802 that the screen arcade and wings of offices were finally completed.

James junior does not say that his father's genius produced one of the architectural gems of Europe. The Irish Bar can consider itself fortunate to practise in such gracious surroundings, particularly by comparison with the Victorian monstrosity in the Strand to which their English brethren are condemned.

It should be added that the building was called the Four Courts because it contained the courts of the four branches of the judicial system, namely, the Courts of Chancery, King's Bench, Exchequer and Common Pleas. These are sited in the huge circular main hall surmounted by a magnificent gallery and dome which is one of the prominent landmarks of Dublin. In this hall were to be found on any day of term a vociferous throng of counsel, attorneys and litigants, transacting their business, lawful and otherwise, and waiting on their cases to be called.

Contemporaneously with the decision to house these four great courts of justice under the same roof, the Society of the Benchers decided to perform a similar service for themselves, and so we come to the modern King's Inns which was the last, and many think the most exquisite, building to be designed by Gandon. Its erection was in the immemorial tradition of the stormy history of the institution and was not effected without acrimony, delay, intrigue and plain unadulterated swindling until Gandon resigned in disgust, leaving the completion to his pupil, Henry A. Baker, who faithfully carried out his master's plan.

Again we are indebted to the architect's son for an account of the project:

The last public building which Mr. Gandon designed was the King's Inns situated at the upper end of Henrietta Street. The Society of the King's Inns is composed of the Lord Chancellor, the twelve Judges, the Benchers, etc. and although this building was in contemplation for many years the Society experienced great difficulty in procuring a suitable plot of ground to embrace all the objects required, and when after considerable delay the plot was purchased on which it was proposed to erect the building, comprising a part of Constitution Hill, the grounds were so occupied by old houses, racket-courts, and dilapidated premises with their defective titles, that much valuable time elapsed before practical operations could be commenced.
The first stone of the King's Inns was laid by Clare, Lord Chancellor, on the 1st August 1795.
In 1798 some barristers presented a memorial to the Benchers asking that their deposits for chambers be refunded as they understood the building of Inns of Court was abandoned or suspended for an indefinite period.

19

In the same year the premises in Townsend Street were surrendered in favour of a temporary building for accommodation of the Society on the present site.

On the 23rd January 1800 a Committee of Benchers was appointed to seek designs and look into the matter, and Gandon's design was approved and work begun on the foundations of the present building on the 1st August 1800.

Difficulties, due to the hostility of the Lord Chancellor, arose in regard to barristers' chambers as part of the scheme, and despite his death in 1802 they were never overcome, and no chambers were ever built, although plans were prepared by Gandon. He resigned as architect in 1806 giving his reasons in a long memorandum. . . . "the work not advancing as rapidly as desired, owing to lack of funds."

It may be added that this observation of Gandon's cloaks as flagrant a piece of financial finagling, and indeed malversation of funds, as ever disgraced even that corrupt period. The Committee referred to not only succeeded in bringing pressure on the owners of the premises on the site to sell at an under-value, but resold to the Society of Benchers, for which they were trustees, at an outrageously enhanced price. Not content with this chicanery the Honourable gentlemen then proceeded to collect monies from their colleagues at the Bar for the projected chambers which were never built. The memorial of 1798 refers to this little criminal transaction: criminal, because as the records of the Society are silent as to the victims ever being reimbursed, we may infer the obvious conclusion.

Oddly enough, these nefarious proceedings proved ultimately to be a blessing in disguise, as they were directly responsible for the unique working conditions at the Irish Bar which represent the outstanding difference between it and its English counterpart.

In Ireland barristers do not have chambers, but work together in the Law Library which is part of the building of the Four Courts. Here are available all the law reports, English and Irish, as well as all the statutes, books and other legal literature which constitutes the practitioner's stock in trade. The result is that every member is the proprietor of a library which even the most eminent and successful of his English brethren could never hope to own.

There are other less tangible, but even more valuable, assets. In the library desks are allotted, and an inflexible code of etiquette prescribes that even the most junior barrister can invoke the assistance of even the most senior. The latter will immediately lay aside his work and give his advice. Accordingly, a solicitor can send a brief for an opinon to a newly called junior, in the comfortable assurance that even if his nominee does not know the answer, the opinion he will get back will have emanated from someone who does. A further by-product, partly of the system and partly of the size of the country, is that specialization is almost unknown, and it is by no means unusual for a busy counsel to find himself in the criminal, common law, and chancery courts all in the same week, an activity unthinkable in England.

The library itself is only a few yards from the High and Supreme Courts, so that authorities on even the most esoteric point which arises in argument are always available. No member of the public, not even a solicitor, is allowed to pass a chain inside the main door of the Library. At this entrance there is a rostrum presided over by an attendant who has a printed list of practising counsel before him, appropriately annotated with his immediate whereabouts. If a solicitor wishes to consult a barrister he tells this important functionary who then shouts out his name, if he is not in court or absent, and he will come out to the hall.

One other privilege attaches to membership of their institution: this is a limited, but not unimportant, right of sanctuary. Within its sacred precincts a member of the Bar is immune from arrest, or service on him of any legal process. Indeed, stories are told of the subterfuges of process servers masquerading as solicitors' clerks who have lured unwary counsel, averse to paying their tradesmen, from the protection of their stronghold into the hall, there to effect personal service on them with what are misleadingly described as civil bills for debt.

The perils and privileges of the Law Library were, however, three years in the future for the student emerging triumphantly from 'Josie's' office in the King's Inns. During the last two years he would be compelled to attend lectures and eat his dinners in the dining-hall of that noble building.

The course of legal education pursued at the King's Inns, or for that matter at the university, is nicely calculated to unfit the student for the practice of any profession whatsoever, and more especially for that of the Law. It is conceivable that on the completion of his studies he would be qualified to hold a junior brief in one case in a hundred in the Supreme Court or the House of Lords, always assuming that he would not be called on to address the tribunal. It is almost certain that he will never have seen a brief for counsel, or know the difference between a summary summons and a civil bill, both of which he will meet every day of his practising life. It is absolutely certain that he will not have the faintest idea how to cross-examine a reluctant witness or, what is far more artistic and difficult, how to examine a garrulous one. He will, however, be an authority on the rights and duties of Roman mortgatees in the time of Julius Cæsar, and could give a learned disquisition on how the doctrine of springing uses grew up in the mediaeval Courts of Chancery, in blissful ignorance of the fact that if the normal barrister came across a springing use in his practice he would probably duck. Equipped, however, with his recondite knowledge, and having satisfied the Benchers that he is not a parliamentary agent, or engaged in trade, or otherwise an unfit and improper person, he is deemed to be qualified to assert the interests of his fellow men in their lives and property at the Bar of Justice, and is accordingly admitted to practise that noble and learned profession.

The requirement of eating dinners is a relic of the days, which indeed lasted into modern times, when there was no set course of legal study and the embryo barrister was expected to befit himself for his avocation by tasting the Attic salt of the disputations of his elders, and garnering the learned crumbs which dropped from their prandial discourse. Although in latter days the pearls of wisdom he can expect to be cast before him in hall are more likely to relate to next Saturday's prospects at the Curragh, or the latest play in the Abbey, than to a neat application of the Rule in Shelley's Case in a recent motion before a Chancery Judge, the dinners serve both pleasant and useful purposes. For one thing they will, theoretically at any rate, teach him to hold his wine like a gentleman, and for another bring him into an easy and friendly intimacy with the Bench and Bar among whom he will spend his professional life.

For his last two years he must eat four, and may eat six, dinners in each of the four legal terms, Michaelmas, Hilary, Easter and Whit. In 1939 the six dinners cost one pound, or three and fourpence each. For this, the youth with a healthy appetite was regaled with very good soup, fish, such as turbot, brill or salmon, a main course which could consist of game, poultry, beef, lamb and so on, with appropriate vegetables, pudding or fruit, finishing with coffee and excellent cheeses and biscuits, with snuff. The last was popularly reputed to be manufactured from dynamite and gunpowder, but when passed around in its eighteenth century battered silver box it was considered very cowardly to refuse it, although the effects of taking an overdose were often spectacular.

An equally generous provision was made for the thirst of the budding Demosthenes. At his behest the wine waiter supplied him with his choice of a bottle of claret, burgundy or marsala, or a half-bottle of port. As a mess consisted of six students, judicious ordering meant that the diners could have a different wine with each course, finishing with port with the cheese.

This ration is doubled on Grand Night, the second Thursday of each dining term, when, as one might expect, the hall is packed with young gentlemen intent on improving their acquaintance with the blushful Hippocrene. Incidentally, it is not remarkable that coming up to six o'clock, which is dinner time, teetotallers acquire a scarcity value and popularity as dining companions not altogether connected with their scintillating wit or social graces, as their wine allowance falls into a common pool. One remembers the almost miraculous capture one Grand Night of four such *rarae aves*, which meant that the two other enterprising members of the mess had between them the disposal of twelve bottles.

It should also be mentioned that there is an unlimited allowance of beer. This beverage, which is in fact an old Dublin ale of a peculiar and startling potency, is dispensed from a receptacle resembling a kind of de-spouted watering-can by a flunkey in tail coat, knee-breeches and buckled shoes who is prepared to supply it by the gallon, if necessary, on demand. Again, legendary stories have come down to us of awesome feats performed in competitions between the giant and doughty champions of other days, when men were really men, and a member of the Inns who was perpendicular at nine o'clock was considered a disgrace to the profession.

The dining-hall is the *pièce-de-résistance* of a beautiful building. Perhaps the less said about the pictures of the generations of judges the better, but the hall itself is a delight. At the east end of it is a raised dais, or platform, where the Benchers dine, immediately below them are the barristers' tables and then, nearest the door, the students. At precisely six o'clock the Benchers come up the middle of the hall in procession, the diners bowing to them as they pass. Everyone must wear a dark jacket and is gowned and, curiously enough, the proceedings, while convivial, are more rigid than at the English Inns. For instance, smoking even after dinner is strictly forbidden, and there is also an inflexible rule that no Bencher can leave the hall before the last of the students. This not infrequently results in a more or less polite intimation from the major domo that it would be appreciated if the young gentlemen would continue their learned discussions either outside the hall, or in the pub at the corner of Henrietta Street which, as long as legal memory extends, has been known as the Court of Appeal.

This, then, is the atmosphere and tradition with which

the neophyte is inculcated and surrounded. When he has attended all his lectures and passed his examinations, bewigged, begowned and banded, he will join his colleagues in the Benchers' room in the Four Courts when the Honourable Society will admit him to the degree of barrister-at-law. He then betakes himself to the Supreme Court where the Chief Justice in open court formally calls him to the practice of his profession. For the rest of this great day he takes precedence before every other member of the Bar, even the Attorney-General, and has the right to interrupt the proceedings in any Court in Ireland, and peremptorily insist on having his case, or application, heard forthwith. But tomorrow he will find that he is very small fry indeed in a very big pond, even if he can address the most eminent leader on equal terms and by his surname, and speak to solicitors with that restrained and dignified authority which distinguishes a member of the senior branch of the profession of twenty-four hours standing.

# 2

# *Unholy Trinity*

The construction of the Four Courts and the King's Inn at the beginning of the last century symbolized in Ireland the opening of the modern era of the administration of Law, if not always of Justice. Indeed, the quality of judicial integrity for many years was such that could the even-handed goddess have contemplated the torturing of legal principles by Judges intent on the objects of an oppressive administration, to which they owed their places, it would have been unnecessary to veil her eyes; they would have been blinded with tears.

The most notorious heads of the contemporary hierarchy of the Irish Bench in order of precedence were the Earl of Clare, Lord Chancellor, the Earl of Clonmel, Lord Chief Justice of the King's Bench, and the Earl of Norbury, Chief Justice of the Common Pleas. Each of these men had achieved his position of rank and wealth as the reward of a single-minded tenacity in upholding the cause of the suppression of the rights and liberties of-his compatriots. It may be added that in the furtherance of their common design each displayed a unique and individual genius.

Of the three, John Fitzgibbon, Lord Clare, was by far the most able. It is extraordinary that no full biography has yet been written about this truly remarkable man. More than anyone he was responsible, against all the probabilities, in forcing through the Act of Union which begot such deplorable results for both Ireland and England. It was he who imbued the youthful Robert Stewart with those principles which caused him finally to cut his throat in tardy expiation, and made the name of Castlereagh a dirty word in the annals of two peoples. Certainly it is one of the ironical anomalies of history that the pupil rather than the master should largely bear the obloquy of crucifying the freedom of his country.

Strangely, at the outset of his career Fitzgibbon was a protagonist with his schoolfellow, Henry Grattan, of the independence, under the Crown, of that Irish Parliament he was later to destroy. It was only when the latter dedicated himself to the enfranchisement of five-sixths of the nation, arguing that there could be no really independent government that was not representative, that the former threw his surpassing ability against the autonomy of the Lords and Commons of Ireland. This was, paradoxically, not ambivalence, but on the contrary, consistency, for every thought and action of "Black Jack" Fitzgibbon, throughout his life, was conditioned by an innate fear and hatred of the least concession to the majority. Innate is a word peculiarly apposite in this connexion because it was from his immediate antecedents that stemmed his implacable intransigence.

Fitzgibbon's father, as a "vagrant boy", was taken in by a charitable family and educated. When he expressed a vocation for the Church he was sent, as was necessary, to the Continent where, having completed his studies in Divinity, he was ordained a Roman Catholic priest. He then abjured his religion and had himself enrolled as a student of the King's Inns and was duly called to the Irish Bar, where he amassed a considerable fortune. This, together with his new-found principles, he bequeathed to his son who proceeded to make a spectacular use of both.

As an example of the Chancellor's liberal ideas we find him, when Attorney General, defending in Parliament the use and extension of torture as a necessary element in the effective exercise of the legal process. During another session, and in the same capacity, he introduced a bill for the demolition of Roman Catholic chapels and religious houses. It was during the debate on this enlightened measure that he said he would make the Roman Catholics in Ireland as "tame as cats". This observation was never to be forgotten; so much so that at his funeral instead of the more conventional floral tributes his tomb was bestrewn with a shower of dead cats contributed by the citizens of Dublin.

The machinations of the younger Pitt and Castlereagh in effecting a union desired by neither country are too well known to call for a further description. What is not well known is that they would have been utterly frustrated were it not for those of the lately created Earl of Clare. As Lord High Chancellor of Ireland he was in a position of power and patronage almost inconceivable in later times, and so used his great office to seduce the more venal members of the Irish Bar into voting in favour of a Bill which they hitherto opposed.

Oliver Burke describes the manner in which he succeeded in accomplishing this purpose:

To carry this measure it became necessary, above all things, to have the co-operation of the Bar; for the Bar was the only great body in the State that he feared as a serious obstruction to his plans. In its ranks were the most accomplished statesmen, the most formidable debaters, and the most earnest opponents of the Union. The Chancellor, therefore, resolved that they should be won at all hazards; and to accomplish this end, he created a great number of legal offices which they were expected to solicit and by which they would become vassals of the Castle. He doubled the number of bankrupt commissions, revived some offices, created others. In the year 1800, the Irish Parliament died its shameful death! It was bought and sold.

This process of the bargain and sale of liberty was so extensive that O'Neill Daunt, in speaking of the post-Union composition of the Irish Bench, observed that "no less than nine individuals can be named who received that elevation as the price of their political iniquity." Nor does this take into account the numerous and hardly less lucrative legal offices, commissions and sinecures which turned the Four Courts into a centre of administrative rapacity.

The principal architect of the Union did not long survive its passing. Fitzgibbon duly took his seat in the House of Lords, where he immediately attempted in accustomed style to overbear the liberal opposition. He very soon found that the Chancellorship, in what was now a provincial judiciary, conferred no authority in that assembly. In his very first speech he abused his ancestral religion and ridiculed his country. For this he was rebuked by the Lord Chancellor of England, and when he lost his temper and resumed he referred to the opposition as "Jacobins and levellers". This gratuitous insolence was too much for the Duke of Bedford who exclaimed "We would not bear this insult from an equal; how much less shall we endure it from the mouth of an upstart and mushroom nobility!"

Humiliated and mortified by English society, which refused to receive him, he returned to Ireland. There, his spirit broken, he went into a decline and died in January 1802, by a coincidence in the very month that marked the first anniversary of the coming into force of the infamous compact which had so quickly disappointed his ambition.

The political activities of Fitzgibbon have almost completely obscured his memory as Lord Chancellor. In fact, when the issues did not inflame his prejudices he could be a very great judge, and such of his judgements as have come down to us are models of lucid and profound exposition of the law. A similar verdict can be passed on the Earl of Clonmel. There is, however, this difference, that whereas Clare's disservice to his country took place largely in the political arena, Clonmel's was mostly confined to the forensic, where he acted as the judicial instrument of the executive in Dublin Castle.

The origins of John Scott were even more lowly than those of the other contemporary John Scott, the coal merchant's son from Newcastle, who rose to the Lord Chancellorship of England as the Earl of Eldon. Although eventually a rich man, Clonmel did not achieve the opulence of his namesake, but in hypocrisy and double-dealing he surpassed him, which is saying a great deal.

His rise to the bench and earldom has a singular resemblance to that of Fitzgibbon, although he was never to wield anything like his influence. Called to the Bar in 1765, in six years he was a King's Counsel and Member of Parliament for Mullingar. From then on his progress continued to be meteoric. In 1774 we find him Solicitor General and a Privy Councillor; later he was successively promoted Attorney General, Prime Serjeant and, finally, Lord Chief Justice. It should perhaps be noted that the Prime Sergeantcy was an ancient Irish legal office which took precedence over that of the Attorney General, and had been in existence over five hundred years when it was abolished in 1805.

As in the case of the Chancellor, the judgements of the Lord Chief Justice, when the political requirements of the Castle were not involved, were replete with learning and good law; but for the sake of his memory it is unfortunate that, because of his conduct in the very trials in which political passion raged, his name is execrated. These were the great State Trials in the dying years of the eighteenth and the beginning of the nineteenth centuries. No more dramatic cases than these have ever been tried in the tribunals of any country. In the Four Courts, and the ancient criminal court in Green Street, there co-existed in every single one of these Trials the most abject venality on the bench opposed by heroism in the dock. In the jury box there invariably sat twelve hand-picked men who underwent the formality of listening to the perjured testimony of paid informers to give colour to the inevitable verdict of Guilty. At the Bar the treacherous MacNally took his blood money for betraying his own clients, while the courage and eloquence of Curran has ensured that in the eyes of history the condemned are the accusers, and the accusers the condemned.

Over these judicial travesties presided the impressive figure of John Scott, Earl of Clonmel, performing in robes and ermine the functions of the hangman as surely as the hand that adjusted the noose. It is a measure of his subtlety and legal skill that his complicity in the rape of justice is not readily apparent in the State Trial Reports. Every so often they report him as deciding against the Crown on some minor matter of evidence or procedure, but a closer study will show that every point of substance that could be material to the Defence is overridden. It was all done so cleverly, however, that not until the publication of the State Papers in the secret archives of Dublin Castle did the enormity of his judicial conduct, although suspected, stand revealed.

In striking contrast to the Earls of Clare and Clonmel, who in the very measure of the perversion of their dominating genius achieved a kind of appalling greatness, John Toler, First Earl of Norbury, capers about the records of the Law as a grotesque whose antics would have been comic were not their effects so tragic.

In two respects, however, he parallelled his superior brethren. He, too, was sprung from humble beginnings, though not as obscure as those of Scott or Fitzgibbon. His father was from a family planted in County Tipperary under the Cromwellian settlement and, at the time of the birth of his hopeful son, was what was known in the Irish countryside as a "Squireen". Squireen, it should be explained, was a generic term descriptive of a class that led a precarious existence in a zone of social twilight somewhere between the peasantry and the gentry, belonging to neither, despised by both.

Toler also mounted the ladder of legal advancement which an ever grateful Castle supplied to its adherents. He successively held the great offices of Solicitor General and Attorney General before his elevation to the Bench as Chief Justice of the Common Pleas, and the peerage, as Earl of Norbury.

31

The career of Norbury on the bench absolutely defies the expository powers of even the most descriptive writer. The best that can be done is to illustrate it by examples, in the hope that they will, when related to each other, convey some idea of a character which cannot be delineated in words. He was devoid of the most rudimentary feeling for jurisprudence, and combined a parrot-like memory for decided cases, without understanding what they decided, with a perverse talent for misapplying them capriciously which amounted to genius. Daniel O'Connell, who practised extensively before him, described him as a "judicial bully, butcher, and buffoon", and we will see that each of these epithets was richly earned.

The first time that Norbury obtrudes himself on our attention in his judicial capacity was when, as Solicitor General, he presided as acting Judge of Assize in Kildare in the murder trial of one Captain Frazer. Frazer was an officer in a Scotch regiment of fencibles, and one evening, when he was drunk after dinner, he accosted a harmless old man who was mending a cartwheel outside his cottage. He demanded why he was not observing the curfew, and when the old fellow told him he was breaking no law as it was not a proclaimed area, he cut him to pieces with his sabre. It was proved before a coroner's jury, who returned a verdict of Wilful Murder, that he inflicted nineteen wounds, any one of nine of which was fatal.

The gallant captain rode up to court on the morning of the trial preceded by the regimental band—a triumph by anticipation which the event was to warrant. Having heard the absolutely uncontroverted evidence of this flagitious and senseless outrage the bloodthirsty buffoon on the bench, in directing the jury to acquit, delivered himself of a charge which almost annihilates belief. He gave it as his opinion that: "Captain Frazer was a gallant officer who had only made a mistake: that if Dixon was a good man, as he was represented to be, it was well for him to be out of this wicked

world; but if he was as bad as many others in the neighbourhood it was as well for the country to be quit of him."

The singular forensic attributes which he first displayed
when presiding over the Frazer trial came to their full flower
when his lordship's judicial appointment was confirmed. It
is proper to say, however, that the Captain's was one of the
very few acquittals before him. Englishmen, who may have
felt that in Jeffries and Scroggs the ultimate in legal ferocity
had been achieved, will hardly credit that Norbury on the
Irish Bench outdid in tyranny, and contempt for the rule of
law, even those legendary monsters—yet so it was. For
example, while Jeffries' most murderous performances are
associated with the aftermath of the Monmouth rebellion,
Norbury's extended over more than a quarter of a century.
In a time of peace, and during one single Assize, he had the
pleasure of sentencing no fewer than one hundred and
ninety-eight men and women to death. On another circuit
one hundred were capitally tried. Two were acquitted; one,
a soldier, who had murdered a peasant, was pardoned, and
ninety-seven were hanged.

That the expression "pleasure" can be used in a context
which for most judges was an ordeal, might sound far-
fetched; its use, however, is amply justified by his attitude
when he assumed the black cap, examples of which abound.

Once, he prefaced the dreadful formula of the death sentence on a pickpocket convicted of stealing a watch, with :
"Egad, my boy, you made a grab at time and caught
eternity!"

On a similar occasion, which happened to be June 20, a
child who should have been under the care of his mother
begged him, "Ah, My Lord, give me the long day"—this
being an Irishism for a plea for life.

Norbury rejoined, "I am happy to oblige you, I will give
you until tomorrow, the longest day of the year."

No man ever bore another's misfortunes more equably.
For some trivial offence he informed the accused, "The sen-

tence of the Court is that you be flogged from the bank to
the quay——"

The prisoner interrupted him, "Thank you, My Lord, you
have done your worst."

"And back again," retorted Norbury finishing his sentence,
which now became almost certainly one of death.

On the civil side of the Court, Toler's conduct was no less
remarkable. He did not, of course, have the same scope for
sadism, nor would most barristers stand for his bullying, but
he could and did give the freest rein to his grotesquerie. The
result was pure bedlam. Even Clare, who for all his vices was
a lawyer, foresaw something of the kind and was genuinely
shocked when his appointment was mooted. "For God's
sake, make him a bishop, or even an archbishop, but not a
chief justice!"

"What is your calling and occupation, my honest man?"
Toler once asked a witness.

"Please, your Lordship, I keep a racket court."

"Begad, that makes a pair of us," chortled the old repro-
bate, delighted with himself.

For once he spoke the truth. The Court was in a continual
uproar with counsel, witnesses and parties all engaged in a
battle royal, in which laughter, shouting, sophistries and
wrangling created a babel din. Over it all could be heard the
bellows of the empurpled and apoplectic Judge.

Luby gives a good picture of the pantomime that was frequently enacted on the bench when his lordship delivered
judgement:

The judicial zany would next profess to enter more deeply into
the case. He would now throw open his robes, perhaps fling off
his wig and stand up, and pour forth an outlandish, unconnected
jumble of anecdotes of his early life—jokes, partly original,
partly borrowed from "Joe Miller" or other jest books; quota-
tions, not always apposite, but well recited, from Milton or
Shakespeare; sarcasms against defendants' counsel; and possibly
a few allusions to some leading incident that turned up in the
course of the trial. He would then suddenly pull up, puffing and
blowing amidst the laughter of the Bar.

34

His court was always packed with spectators who flocked in as to a performance in the theatre. They were rarely disappointed, for when the principal clown came waddling in all decorum vanished and it became a bear-garden.

Not even cases involving the most serious, indeed tragic, issues were immune from his ribald treatment. A famous instance was the case of Guthrie v. Sterne where the defendant had undergone the most terrible chastisement from the tongue of Charles Phillips, the Plaintiff's counsel, for seducing his client's wife. The Courts always affected an appearance of shocked outrage at evidence of this sort of activity. Having regard to the private lives of the incumbents of the Bench, and the liberal interpretation of the binding force of the marriage vow by contemporary society in general, we may assume that this attitude was a pleasant legal fiction. But Guthrie's was a truly sad case as a hitherto happy family life had been irreparably destroyed.

The atmosphere of solemnity was dispelled in short order when Chief Justice Norbury briefly summed up for the benefit of the jury. Having fixed the Defendant with a stare that made him wilt, he turned to the jury: "Gentlemen, I will refrain from elaborating on the Defendant's character which (if I may be permitted a nautical expression) has been raked fore and aft and from stem to stern by Mr. Phillips. I will, therefore, content myself with observing in regard to Mr. William Peter Baker Dunstanville Sterne that had he been in possession of as many Christian virtues as Christian names, he would have neither embarked on 'Sterne's Sentimental Journey' nor been guilty of the revolting crime of seduction."

There were few occasions for laughter, however, when his lordship exercised his criminal jurisdiction, and certainly none in the terrible miscarriage of justice effected in the trial of Philip Barry for highway robbery. As this case is unique in the annals of judicial malignancy it deserves to be treated at some length.

The accused, to Norbury's knowledge, had been brought the day before to Kilkenny from the previous assize town,

Clonmel, to stand his trial for this capital offence. His counsel, Burrowes Campbell, accordingly asked for an adjourn-
ment to obtain his witnesses, and although the prosecution
did not object the judge postponed the case only until the
following morning. This, having regard to the distance and
travelling conditions, was useless, and what then transpired
was later sworn to on oath by Burrowes Campbell: "I then
drew Barry's affidavit (as to his witnesses) and moved on it."

"Did any magistrate of the name of Elliott interfere?"

"Yes: he was sitting in the bar-box when one of the Bar
mentioned to me that he (Mr. Elliott) knew three of the
parties mentioned in the affidavit. I asked Mr. Elliott in open
court if these parties resided at the distance stated, and he
said they did. I, therefore, moved a postponement to enable
my client to procure their attendance, but the judge thought
proper to refuse the motion.

"I told the judge that I would not go through the mockery
of a trial, when I knew the man had not his witnesses, and
that if the trial were called on, his lordship should defend
the man himself. I accordingly threw up my brief and left
the court."

"On what grounds did the judge refuse the application by
affidavit?"

"He said that if a trial were to be postponed upon an
affidavit as complete and professionally drawn, prisoners
would only have to employ counsel to draw an affidavit when
they wished to put off their trials. I asked his lordship what
he would have said if the affidavit had been defective."

"Did you, after the conviction of this unfortunate man,
make an application to the judge who tried him in order to
obtain mercy?"

"After the conviction I wrote a respectful letter to Lord
Norbury, enclosing the voluntary affidavits of those persons
who were known to be Barry's witnesses, in which they swore
that he was in their company at a distance of forty-five miles
when the robbery was committed! To this I never received
any answer . . . I then applied to the Attorney General."

36

"Were there any other grounds?" (for the application to the judge and later to the Attorney General).

"I made it on the grounds of two affidavits—the one made by James Rodgers and three other persons named in the affidavits sworn to postpone the trial, stating that on the day charged in the indictment the convict Patrick Barry was in their company at Kilcannon at the distance of forty or fifty miles from the place where the alleged robbery was committed, and that they never heard of his being accused of the robbery until after his trial."

"Did you mention the circumstances to any person?"

"I did. I talked publicly of it in the hall of the Four Courts, and told it to everyone I met, and to every gentleman of the Bar with whom I was acquainted."

"In what manner did you speak of it?"

"I always spoke of it as a most shocking event."

"Are you of opinion that the conduct of the Judge was a fit subject for Parliamentary inquiry?"

"I am; and I did at the time think so, and repeatedly said so."

Despite this "most shocking event", about as flagrant an example of premeditated judicial murder as history affords, the Attorney General, Saurin, ignored Campbell's representations, and Norbury continued his atrocious career on the bench until, in Canning's Prime Ministry in 1827, he was induced to resign with a pension of £3,046.

Two years previously a petition had been drawn up calling for Norbury's removal on the grounds that he had fallen asleep during a murder trial and was unable to give an account of the evidence when his notes were called for by the Lord Lieutenant. Peel assured the House that the matter would be inquired into but nothing was done.

At last, on July 27 1831, the old scoundrel died in Dublin at the age of eighty-five. Even on his death-bed his penchant for bad puns did not desert him. On hearing that his neighbour, Lord Erne, was also fatally ill, he called his valet:

37

"James, run around to Lord Erne and tell him with my compliments that it will be a dead heat between us."

It was, appropriately, a butcher's apprentice who delivered his panegyric.

When they were burying him the grave was so deep that the ropes lowering the coffin did not reach the bottom. It remained hanging half-way while somebody was sent for more rope.

"Ay," said the butcher's lad, "give him rope enough, don't stint him! He was the boy that never grudged it to anybody when he was alive."

# 3

# *Nor Law,*
# *nor Duty . . .*

The Irish Judiciary at the opening of the modern legal era was an institution of almost unexampled venality; particularly in asserting the powers of the establishment over the rights of the citizen. This does not imply that they were not men of learning and ability; in fact, most of them were both and frequently displayed these qualities when the case did not involve the Government. Nor is it a comprehensive indictment. There were exceptions.

For example, Lord Kilwarden, Chief Justice of the King's Bench and a friend of Curran's, was described by him as "an excellent and humane judge who had saved many an innocent prisoner from death". It was a tragic irony that in the Emmett rebellion, alone of all the judges, poor old Kilwarden was murdered, and a monster like Norbury was not even molested.

No such generalization can be made about the Bar who practised before the judges. Here we find exhibited almost every quality which human nature can display, from the courageous eloquence of Curran through the ferocity of Saurin to the abyss of treachery as personified in Leonard MacNally.

There was one quality which was common to all of them and which more than any other distinguished them, not only from their English brethren, but from all but the most reckless in a notoriously fire-eating society. This was a punctilio as to what was conceived to be the point of honour, and was so nice as to have a flash-point even lower than the powder with which their duelling pistols were primed. It was no more than the literal truth that no barrister could be received on terms of equality by his colleagues in the Four Courts unless he had proved his mettle at least once in an honourable encounter.

Some idea of the hazards which attended the practice of law may be derived from a study of the code of duelling— which reflects great credit on the draughtsmanship of its framers. This historic document was drawn at the Lent Assizes in Galway and accepted at the Summer Assizes in Clonmel in 1777, and was thereafter of binding force and effect. It is designed to cover all but the most *outré* cases, which could be referred by either second to a specially convened Court of Honour. It deserves to be reproduced in full:

*Rules as to Duelling and Points of Honour*
1. The first offence requires the first apology, though the retort may have been more offensive than the insult.
Example. A tells B he is impertinent etc., B retorts that he lies; yet A must make the first apology, because he gave the first offence, and then, after one fire, B may explain away the retort by subsequent apology.
2. But if the parties would rather fight on, then, after two shots each, but in no case before, B may explain first, and A apologise afterwards.
N.B. The above rules apply to all cases of offences in retort not of a stronger class than the example.
3. If a doubt exist who gave the first offence, the decision rests with the seconds; if they won't decide or can't agree, the matter must proceed to two shots, or to a hit, if the challenge require it.
4. When the *lie direct* is the first offence, the aggressor must either beg pardon in express terms, exchange two shots previous to apology, or three shots followed up by explanation, or fire on till a severe hit be received by one party or the other.
5. As a blow is strictly prohibited under any circumstances amongst gentlemen, no verbal apology can be received for such

an insult: the alternatives, therefore, are, the offender handing a cane to the injured party, to be used on his own back, at the same time begging pardon, firing on until one or both is disabled, or exchanging three shots, and then asking pardon, *without* the proffer of the cane.

If swords are used, the parties engage till one is well blooded, disabled or disarmed; or until, after receiving a wound, and blood being drawn, the aggressor begs pardon.

N.B. A *disarm* is considered the same as *disable*: the disarmer may strictly break his adversary's sword; but if it be the challenger who is disarmed, it is considered as ungenerous to do so.

In case the challenged be disarmed and refuses to ask pardon or atone, he must not be *killed*, as formerly; but the challenger may lay his own sword on the aggressor's shoulder, then break the aggressor's sword, and say, "I spare your life!" The challenged can never revive that quarrel—the challenger may.

6. If A gives B the lie, and B retorts by a blow, being the two greatest offences, no reconciliation can take place till after two discharges each, or a severe hit; *after* which B may beg A's pardon humbly for the blow, and then A may explain simply for the lie; because a blow is *never* allowable, and the offence of the lie therefore merges in it. (See preceding rule.)

N.B. Challenges for undivulged causes may be reconciled on the ground, after one shot. An explanation or the slightest hit should be sufficient in such cases, because no personal offences transpired.

7. But no apology can be received in any case after the parties have actually taken their ground, without exchange of fires.

8. In the above case no challenger is obliged to divulge his cause of challenge, if private, unless required by the challenged so to do *before* their meeting.

9. All imputations of cheating at play, races, etc., to be considered equivalent to a blow, but may be reconciled after one shot, on admitting their falsehood, and begging pardon publicly.

10. Any insult to a lady under a gentleman's care or protection to be considered as, by one degree, a greater offence than if given to the gentleman personally, and to be regulated accordingly.

11. Offences originating or accruing from the support of ladies' reputations to be considered as less unjustifiable than any others of the same class, and as admitting of slighter apologies by the aggressor—this to be determined by the circumstances of the case, but *always* favourable to the lady.

12. In simple unpremeditated *rencontres* with the small sword, or *couteau-de-chasse*, the rule is—first draw, first sheathe; unless blood be drawn, then both sheathe, and proceed to investigation.

13. No dumb-shooting or firing in the air admissible *in any case*. The challenger ought not to have challenged without receiving

offence; and the challenged ought, if he gave offence, to have made an apology before he came on the ground; therefore *children's play* must be dishonourable on one side or the other, and is accordingly prohibited.

14. Seconds to be of equal rank in society with the principals they attend, inasmuch as a second may either choose or chance to become a principal, and equality is indispensable.

15. Challenges are never to be delivered at night, unless the party to be challenged intends leaving the place of offence before morning; for it is desirable to avoid all hot-headed proceedings.

16. The challenged has the right to choose his own weapon, unless the challenger gives his honour he is no swordsman; after which, however, he cannot decline any *second* species of weapon proposed by the challenged.

17. The challenged chooses his ground; the challenger chooses his distance; the seconds fix the time and terms of firing.

18. The seconds load in presence of each other, unless they give their mutual honours they have charged smooth and single, which should be held sufficient.

19. Firing may be regulated—first, by signal; secondly, by word of command; or thirdly, at pleasure, as may be agreeable to the parties. In the latter case, the parties may fire at their reasonable leisure, but *second presents* and *rests* are strictly prohibited.

20. In all cases a miss-fire is equivalent to a shot, and a *snap* or a *non-cock* is not to be considered as a miss-fire.

21. Seconds are bound to attempt a reconciliation *before* the meeting takes place, or *after* sufficient firing or hits, as specified.

22. Any wound sufficient to agitate the nerves, and necessarily make the hand shake, must end the business for *that day*.

23. If the cause of the meeting be of such a nature that no apology or explanation can or will be received, the challenged takes his ground, and calls on the challenger to proceed as he chooses; in such cases firing at pleasure is the usual practice, but may be varied by agreement.

24. In slight cases the second hands his principal but one pistol, but in gross cases two, holding another case ready-charged in reserve.

25. Where seconds disagree, and resolve to exchange shots themselves, it must be at the same time and at right angles with their principals, thus:

```
           S
           |
           |
P——————|——————P
           |
           |
           S
```

If with swords, side by side, with five paces interval.
N.B. All matters and doubts not herein mentioned will be explained and cleared up by application to the committee, who meet alternately at Clonmel and Galway, at the Assizes for that purpose.

CROW RYAN, *President*
JAMES KEOGH, ⎫ *Secretaries*
AMBY BODKIN, ⎭

*Additional Galway Articles*
1. No party can be allowed to bend his knee or cover his side with his left hand, but may present at any level from the hip to the eye.
2. None can either advance or retreat if the ground be measured. If no ground be measured, either party may advance at his pleasure, even to touch muzzle; but neither can advance on his adversary after the fire, unless the adversary steps forward on him.
N.B. The seconds on both sides stand responsible for this last rule being *strictly* observed, bad cases having accrued from neglecting it.

This elaborate code was not only binding on the Bar but also on the Bench. Fitzgibbon fought several duels when a Judge, and Clonmel was reputed one of the best shots of his time. In fact, both these adornments of the Bench had the distinction of engaging with the notorious "Fighting" Fitz-Gerald (who fought more than seventy duels, and was eventually hanged with his attorney at Castlebar). What is more singular, and we may feel, unfortunate, is that both gentlemen escaped from these adventures unscathed.

Norbury, as might be expected, was an inveterate duellist, and even when presiding over the Common Pleas, he would indulge his bloody-mindedness by attacking counsel, there being no unfortunate prisoner available in the dock.

On one occasion he addressed an advocate who was obnoxious to him in these judicious and judicial terms:

"How dare you address me so, Sir. Have a care, Sir, and do not think for one moment that I will hide the gentleman behind the robe of the judge."

Even the written pleadings of counsel were liable to give rise to deadly offence. There was a process known as demurrer which was particularly dangerous to make as it entailed impugning the validity of one's opponent's pleadings and hence his legal competence, thereby frequently leading to an interchange of shots. We are told that any client so head-strong as to call for taxation of his attorney's bill of costs left himself open to either a horsewhipping or a bullet, depending on his social status.

As to the social cachet conferred on the practitioner by fighting a duel, Sir Jonah Barrington tells us that he fought MacNally out of pity. It seems that the infamous Leonard, when admitted to the Bar, was so contemptible in the eyes of his colleagues, both by reason of the vulgarity of his conduct and his insanitary habits, that they consistently refused to honour him by either calling him out or accepting a challenge. Barrington, out of his kindness of heart, consented to meet him and shot him in the thigh, thereby conferring on him a permanent limp and a place in the society of his fellows.

When one considers the powers of invective of the counsel of the day, it is surprising that any of them died in his bed, as witness an extract from a speech by Henry Grattan. In referring to one by Isaac Corry, a fellow barrister, delivered under the protection of Parliamentary privilege, he declaimed that if it were elsewhere: "I should answer only with a blow. I care not how high his situation, how low his character, how contemptible his speech, whether a privy counsellor or a parasite, my answer would be a blow. The right honourable gentleman has told me I deserted a profession where wealth and station were the reward of industry and talent. If I mistake not, that gentleman endeavoured to obtain those rewards by the same means; but he soon deserted the occupation of a barrister for those of a parasite and pander. He fled from the labour of the study to flatter at the table of the great. He found the lord's parlour a better sphere for his exertions than the hall of the Four Courts; the house of a great man a more convenient way to power and to place; and that it was easier for a statesman of middling talents to sell his friends than for a lawyer of no talents to sell his clients."

This was but a portion of a terrible Phillipic which led to a duel in which Corry was wounded.

The genius of Grattan was largely reserved for Parliament, that of Curran for the Courts. It was a period when the art of oratory, a necessary accomplishment of every successful advocate, was also extremely dangerous. It brought John Philpot Curran into deadly combat on several occasions, two of which are notable. The first of these was with Fitzgibbon when Attorney General, and the second with Captain St. Leger, cousin of Lord Doneraile, as a result of a case in which Curran rightly gave both the Captain and his lordship grounds to invoke practically every article of the Code of Duelling.

Curran was the supreme advocate in the history of the Irish Bar, whose reputation rests on as secure a basis as that of his great counterpart in England, Thomas Erskine. Like Erskine he was utterly fearless in his defence of the liberty of the subject against the executive; unlike him, his advocacy frequently brought him into actual personal danger, both in and out of Court. It is almost unbelievable that in such circumstances his closest associate in the great State Trials should have been the infamous Leonard MacNally. The greatest tribute to the latter's consummate genius for his double role is that never for a moment in their long association did the great advocate ever suspect his junior of selling the very clients for whom he appeared to fight so hard.

From no account of the Irish Bar, however superficial, can the career of MacNally be omitted. Of whatever other faults or vices its members may have been guilty, of one no other has ever been accused. Whenever a barrister accepted a criminal brief the interests of the accused, and his alone, henceforward became paramount. Subject to good faith with the law and the court, no other consideration could be allowed to operate to the detriment of the prisoner, and this even included the placing of counsel's professional career in jeopardy if necessary.

This rule is as rigid to-day as ever; it entails "following your prisoner" until every legal remedy is exhausted, and putting aside any other work which interferes with the case. No admission can be made by the defence in a criminal case and so on—the whole code of ethics having for its object the vindication of the innocence of the accused until the contrary be proved. Although there have been several examples, some quite recent, of counsel exceeding his duties and privileges in an excessive zeal for his client's interests, other than in the atrocious career of MacNally, there has never been a single instance when they have been betrayed. In furnishing these instances Leonard Edward MacNally, Barrister-at-Law, stands alone on a monument of unique enormity.

He was born in Dublin in 1752, and having studied in the Middle Temple was called to the English and Irish Bars. When in London he devoted himself for some years to journalism and writing for the stage. He wrote one Drury Lane success, *Robin Hood*, and the song *Sweet Lass of Richmond Hill*, but he made no headway at the English Bar, despite saving the life of Dr. Thurlow, the Lord Chancellor's brother, during the Gordon Riots, and representing Charles James Fox at a Westminster election. He returned to Ireland in penury, and before he could try his luck at the Irish Bar was forced to open a grocery shop in the not very salubrious Mary's Lane, to support a young wife and family.

At this stage of his life it is hard to withhold one's pity from him. He was socially ostracized by his legal brethren in the Four Courts and treated with contempt. When he remarked to a colleague in the Law Library, "Did you hear about my son's robbery?" the reply was, "Really, whom did he rob?" His professional struggles went unrewarded; even the United Irishmen, of whose Society he was one of the first members, regarded him with suspicion. This attitude was typical of that ill-starred body, whose groundless mistrust

46

when he was incorrupt only altered to unquestioning confidence when MacNally had, in fact, become its Judas.

As a practising member of the Irish Bar he first brought himself into prominence by his able advocacy on behalf of Napper Tandy—the same immortalized in *The Wearin' of the Green*. As a result of this case he attracted the sympathy and patronage of Curran. This association ensured his acceptance into the newly formed United Irishmen, because although Curran abhorred violence—except on the duelling ground—and was never a member, his patriotism and integrity were unimpeachable.

As far as can be discovered, no suggestion of duplicity can be made against MacNally in the beginning but in 1794, arriving at the parting of the ways, he chose the one which led to infamy.

The circumstances which led to his terrible dilemma would be incredible in a novel. In 1793, after the execution of Louis XVI, England declared a war on France that did not end for twenty-two years. The invasion of an overwhelmingly friendly Ireland at once became the dream of every French (and the nightmare of every English) government, until the exile of Napoleon to Saint Helena.

In 1794, the exploration of the possibilities of a descent on Irish shores was entrusted to one William Jackson, a Church of England curate, by the French. Almost the first person in London to whom the inept parson confided his mission was a miscreant attorney called Cockayne who immediately informed Pitt. That devious politician instructed Cockayne to go to Dublin with Jackson, although he did not tell him that he was sending another spy to watch the informer himself. In Dublin Jackson and Cockayne were entertained by Mac-Nally who introduced them to the most prominent United Irishmen, and arranged for them to visit Hamilton Rowan who was serving a sentence for seditious libel.

With almost unbelievable rashness a detailed assessment of the prospects for invasion was introduced into the prison by Jackson. Rowan prepared several copies which miraculously were not captured, and gave one to Jackson who in turn made others, thoughtfully giving one to Cockayne.

Within the week Jackson was arrested for high treason.

The Government had now enough evidence to hang, draw and quarter MacNally any time they liked, and well he knew it. We do not know whether he was approached by the Government, or it by him—probably the former. We do know, however, that by the time of Jackson's trial he had made a choice from which there could never be a turning back. This choice was quite simply between a life sentence to corruption, perfidy, and betrayal, and death upon that scaffold on which hundreds of his countrymen suffered directly or indirectly through his treachery.

MacNally did not hesitate, and from the time he had taken the irrevocable step his career assumes a kind of fantastic hellishness. At its very outset, having disclosed to the Castle all of Jackson's transactions, he proceeded to act as his counsel. After the verdict Jackson bravely took poison and died dramatically in the dock before Clonmel could pass sentence of death for high treason. This act preserved his property for his family, which would otherwise be forfeit to the Crown. He had appointed MacNally his executor and had given him his will and a report to the French Convention. Before the body was cold both documents had been copied in Dublin Castle.

Soon, deep in the confidence of the patriot party, MacNally was the fearless and unsullied advocate by day and the informer for blood-money by night. In the trials of the period his brilliant speeches, in which he denounced the contrived evidence, the packed juries and the Government spies, were worthy of Curran himself, whose son said he regarded him to the day he died "with the most uncompromising and romantic fidelity". Had his great leader known that his junior, for a pension of £300 per annum (the rate for Green Street being higher than for Gethsemane) reported to the Castle on all his transactions, even giving them copies of his briefs, he would hardly have embraced him with tears in his eyes, as he did after the condemnation of their client, Peter Finnerty, when he said to him: "My old and excellent friend, I have long known and respected the honesty of your heart, but never until this occasion was I acquainted with the extent of your abilities."

He was counsel for Robert Emmet, and a few days before the trial received £100. Later in the year, when his client had been hanged, drawn and quartered in Thomas Street, his grateful employers conferred on him an extra bonus of £1,000. In this case the ineffable MacNally may be said to have displayed his virtuosity in its full luxuriance. He sat scornfully facing Norbury on the bench as Emmet finished his speech from the dock: "I am ready to die—I have not been allowed to vindicate my character; I have but one request to ask at my departure from this world—it is the charity of its silence. Let no man write my epitaph, for as no man who knows my motives dares to vindicate them, let not prejudice or ignorance asperse them. Let them rest in obscurity and peace; my memory be left in oblivion and my tomb remain uninscribed, until other times and other men can do justice to my character. When my country takes its place among the nations of the earth then, and not till then, let my epitaph be written."

This immortal peroration so affected his counsel that when Norbury had sentenced the prisoner to be hanged, beheaded and disembowelled, MacNally rushed to the dock, threw his arms around Emmet's neck and kissed him. The following morning he was the last to see him in prison before the execution cart arrived. He spoke of Emmet's mother who, unknown to the prisoner, had died some days before.

"How I should love to see her now," Emmet said.

MacNally silently pointed to the sky: "You will see her to-night."

Among Emmet's farewell letters was one to his brother giving a full account of the preparations for the recent rising. He gave them all to Leonard who delivered them, after they had been duly recorded in the secret archives of Dublin Castle.

He had faithfully earned his thousand pounds.

This was the highlight of his career. After Emmet the spirit of rebellion languished and although the Government continued his pension, his services were in small demand. In 1807, when Master of the Rolls, the unsuspecting Curran attempted through his friend the Duke of Bedford to have him called within the bar. Curran was mystified when His Grace shortly informed him that he was powerless.

He did not tell him that in regard to a silk gown for Mac-Nally, Sir Arthur Wellesley, later Duke of Wellington, had written to Mr. Trail, a member of the Irish Government: "I entirely agree with you respecting the employment of our informer. Such a measure would do much mischief. It would disgust the loyal of all descriptions; at the same time it would render useless our private communication with him, as no further trust would be placed in him by the disloyal."

Curran never knew about MacNally, because it was not until his death in 1820 that proof of the arch-informer's treachery stunned the public. This was because of the almost inconceivable temerity of his family in petitioning the Government for the reversion of the pension, which it need hardly be said was refused with the same contempt as it had originally been paid. Further, its recipient having literally outlived his usefulness, the Castle authorities saw no reason to keep secret the circumstances of the original grant, so everything came to light.

MacNally's own son pronounced his epitaph. When his father lay dying, and in despair asked for a Catholic priest so that he could be reconciled to the faith he had so long abandoned, his filial child observed: "Let him go to Hell his own way!"

# 4

# *Tongues to Persuade*

To suggest that Clare, Clonmell, or Norbury were typical of the Irish Bench at the turn of the nineteenth century would convey a distorted impression. This triumvirate were venal to the last degree, but among their successors, always excepting the Union Judges, the majority discharged their functions impartially according to their lights. Unfortunately for the administration of justice in Ireland these lights were lit in London, whence they were appointed. The Judges on the Irish Bench, certainly in the superior courts, were men who, however well disposed, were out of touch with, or antipathetic to, Irish customs and the native genius. Promoted through Government favour for the greater part of the century, if they were not English they were recruited from the ascendancy class. For example, the greatest legal office, the Lord Chancellorship, of immense influence and patronage, in the appointment of puisne judges, magistrates and legal functionaries generally was a plum invariably reserved to an Englishman for services rendered. Its incumbency by such learned nincompoops as Lord St. Leonards, or Mitford, first Baron Redesdale, confirmed

51

the Irish in the view that the Law was a foreign and incongruous institution.

Furthermore, throughout the century the story of the country is lamentable. For Ireland, the sixty glorious years of Victoria are remembered as the period during which the population declined from more than eight millions to a little over four, and her late Majesty, in the words of the Dublin joxer, as "the oul' trollop that gev fifty quid to the Dublin Cat and Dogs Home, and a fiver for the relief of the starvin' poor." The iniquitous land system was, of course, the root cause from which flowed misery, famine and evictions with the attendant evils of coercive laws, followed by retaliation entailing yet more coercion in a vicious concentric progression like the disturbed surface of a polluted pond. All this had its repercussions in the courts, the time of which was, both on the criminal and civil sides, to a large extent devoted to the decision of cases arising out of an agrarian imbroglio in which the interests of three quarters of the people clashed head-on with those of the Establishment.

An appreciation of this last fact is fundamental to an understanding of the outlook of the Irish on the Law. Whereas the average Englishman, at any rate in the last century, regarded it as the bastion of his liberties, despite the onslaughts of such as Dickens in *Bleak House*, the average Irishman regarded it as an instrument of oppression. Not once during the entire century was an Englishman deprived of the protection of the Habeas Corpus Act; in Ireland suspension by enactment after enactment caused the periods of its operation to pass almost unnoticed.

Again, the statute to which the petty magistracy had continual recourse was the Riot Act. In this procedure they had the full approbation of the authorities as personified by such as Arthur Balfour (known in England as the "gentlest of Prime Ministers", and in Ireland, when Chief Secretary, as "Bloody Balfour") who gave the constabulary the gentle direction "Do not hesitate to shoot!" It is hardly surprising, therefore, that most Irishmen regarded the Law, whether as litigant or accused, witness or juror, with an ineradicable antagonism and suspicion, and this was especially true of the country parts.

It should be said, however, that this attitude co-existed with a passionate sense of justice, and it was only the persuasion, rightly or wrongly, that an Irishman was called on to assist in the execution of an unjust code that caused him so often to assume a protective armour of evasiveness, ingenious trickery and downright perjury. This reaction to the administration of justice became so conditioned that it manifested itself even in cases free from the remotest tinge of political or social significance.

Having regard to this ingrained aversion to the system, it might well be concluded that the Irish avoided the Courts like the plague. The direct contrary is the fact, and it can be safely asserted that there certainly was, and probably is, no more litigious race on the face of the earth. For this seeming paradox there were many reasons. First, was the fact that in the countryside most disputes had to do directly or indirectly with land. From the land came the countryman's livelihood, indeed his life, so that the least interference with a right of way, or the trespass of an animal, was an intolerable threat to security. Similarly, actions over wills and settlements, marriage compacts and contracts generally, when analysed would usually be found to have their roots firmly embedded in the land. The Court lists were accordingly packed with cases of a type and variety that in England would never see the light of day.

A hardly less compelling factor in the Irish love of litigation—as distinct from love of the Law—is a highly developed sense of the dramatic. Nearly every Irishman is a born actor, and nowhere is this more evident than in a court of law. To witness a farmer giving evidence in a case involving, for instance, breach of warranty of a cow, is a histrionic experience. From the moment he takes the oath, creating for the unwary the illusion that he intends to observe it, the Court becomes a stage for an accomplished performance by a virtuoso. His own counsel is answered with a manly air of rectitude, his opponent's with an almost pitying contempt, while the judge is addressed with voluble, invariably courteous, explanation. One's admiration is so enlisted that the fact that he has not uttered one syllable of truth seems almost irrelevant.

If civil cases in Ireland often assume a character that would astonish the normally stolid Englishman who, it has been said, "prefers his law dull", it is in criminal trials that this character achieves its apotheosis. At any time, and in any country, a criminal trial is charged with the highest drama. During the last century when liberty, even life, could be imperilled by a trivial transgression, every weapon in the extensive armoury of the prosecution and the defence was brought to bear, and the Irish courts became arenas for really crucial battles of wits in which the most usual casualty was Justice.

The principal warriors in these engagements were, of course, the members of the Bar who, because of the forensic tradition in which they were bred, had developed a style of advocacy so distinctive as to be unique. This style, easier to recognize than dissect, was, as occasion demanded, composed of wit and humour, bullying and sarcasm, cajolery and pathos, to all of which were attuned the sensitive ears of a critical audience. Above all, an Irish jury demanded oratory.

It is impossible to exaggerate the effects which could be produced on a gathering of Irishmen by the exercise of this most meritricious of the arts. Highly articulate themselves, they admired, after courage, no greater quality in a man than the gift of persuasion. It might almost be said that Daniel O'Connell possessed no other mastery over the people than the magic of his tongue, yet they assembled from the four provinces of the country by hundreds of thousands merely to hear him. They would have followed him to death had he spoken the word.

So it was in the courts, and so highly regarded was this accomplishment that we find the earliest discipline of such as Curran and Plunkett, Bushe and Sheil, and a hundred successors, was the study of Cicero and Demosthenes, or the declamation before the mirror of passages from such models as Shakespeare, Bolingbroke or Junius.

Nor was this sort of oratory reserved for the great occasion; an Irishman's sense of the ludicrous being what it is, his afflatus is as often the offspring of the comic as of the tragic muse. It is unfortunate that in the nature of things the vast majority of recorded speeches have been those in grave and weighty proceedings involving the most solemn issues, to the neglect of other juristic *tours-de-force*, no less brilliant because inspired by lighter themes.

Happily for the gaiety of legal annals the balance is somewhat restored by the address to the jury of counsel for the defendant in the deathless case of Blake v. Wilkins.

The facts of this case were remarkable enough in themselves, but Charles Phillips' speech to the jury confers on it an immortality which ranks it in legal history with Bardell v. Pickwick, in fiction.

The heroine of this celebrated cause, which is invariably known as the Widow Wilkins case, was an aged lady living in retirement on her extensive estates in County Galway, bequeathed by her husband. Many visitors to seaside boarding houses will have pleasant memories of an oleograph which at one time was almost as ubiquitous a feature of their adornment as the castor-oil plant. This depicted General Wolfe artistically expiring on the Heights of Abraham in the arms of a fellow officer. This latter gentleman was Surgeon-Major Wilkins, the husband of the lady who was later to immortalize his name.

In the days of her youth her charms were so manifest as to captivate no less an admirer than George III, and at a Court levée his majesty monopolized the company of the beauteous Wilkins for a full hour. Alas! that was long ago and in the very year that she conquered London society, her husband died of a fever. The disconsolate widow retired to her mansion at Brownville in Galway, where she led the life of a

55

recluse for forty years until her fortunes became entangled with those of her designing neighbours, the Blakes.

The Blakes were a family of considerable antiquity, indeed nobility, in the west of Ireland but at this juncture their fortunes were very much in decline. The family consisted of the mother, daughter and son, Peter, who was a personable but contriving naval lieutenant of twenty-three, unsuccessfully attempting to make ends meet on his half-pay of £50 a year. Peter had been an officer on board his majesty's frigate *Hydra*, and had twice circumnavigated the globe in her. The year 1815 saw the final overthrow, not only of the fortunes of Napoleon, but also those of a great number of Peter's profession when the huge fleets which had strangled Bonaparte were laid aside, and their personnel with them.

An able bodied and unemployable young man around the house very quickly sheds his heroic aura, and after a year or two the female Blakes decided that drastic measures would have to be taken. Their roving eye alighted on their wealthy and decrepit neighbour.

The siege of the widow commenced with the most pressing invitations, which soon became matters of routine, to enjoy hospitality on as lavish a scale as their straitened means could afford. Insensibly, the old lady began to regard herself as almost one of the family. She was encouraged to talk by the hour about her conquest of London and King George in the far off halcyon days. When she spoke of the marital bliss which she enjoyed with the incomparable surgeon-major, the ladies delicately suggested that it was far from too late to replace even that paragon by another who would bring her undreamt of happiness, such as she had never known.

Gradually, the notion of repairing her single state was implanted in the mind of the poor old victim, and through the insidious suggestions of the female Blakes, and the most revolting flattery of the gallant lieutenant, she allowed herself to be ensnared into a promise of marriage. No sooner was the engagement effected than she fell completely into the clutches of the three conspirators. She was cut off from her own relatives, and even her freedom of movement was restricted. The precious trio must have overplayed their hand, however, because in a moment of lucidity the old lady called off the connexion and got in touch with her trustees, who in turn got in touch with their solicitors; they wrote in the strongest terms to Peter who replied by issuing a writ.

And so was born the famous case of Blake v. Wilkins.

No case before or since, certainly no civil case, aroused such excitement in Galway. From all parts of Connaught the west descended on the city in their thousands. For a whole week before the case it was impossible to rent even a bed, and the correspondent for the *Freeman's Journal* informs us, "Three of us slept in one bed last night, and four in the other; it was like the black hole of Calcutta."

Baron Smith of the Exchequer was the presiding judge, and the plaintiff was represented by no fewer than four counsel, the defendant by three.

Mr. Crampton opened the pleadings, which consisted of a variety of counts through which ran a lowest common denominator which expressed in the clearest and most forcible terms that the plaintiff claimed £5,000 as a measure of the injury to his feelings, outraged by the breach of promise of the heartless widow.

Thomas Vandeleur, K.C., set out the plaintiff's case, called his evidence and then it was the turn of the defendant. Daniel O'Connell had been brought down to lead the defence team, but as a victim of the convivial hospitality of the Connaught Bar the previous night, he found that when he attempted to use his voice he could produce nothing more intelligible than a sepulchral croak. The duty of conducting the defence unexpectedly devolved upon his junior who made such a triumph of it that he was thereafter known as the "silver-tongued" Phillips. This volatile gentleman, having determined to laugh the case out of court, flew in the face of all legal convention and levelled the artillery of his ridicule at his own client.

The speech is a miracle of extempore, and the excerpts

which follow will give some idea of the whole, which runs to several pages of a contemporary pamphlet.

His unfortunate client had the pleasure of listening to her counsel observe to the jury "How vainglorious is the boast of beauty! How misapprehended have been the claims of youth, if years and wrinkles can thus despoil their conquests and depopulate the navy of its prowess, and beguile the bar of its eloquence! How mistaken were all the amatory poets, from Anacreon downwards, who preferred the bloom of the rose and the trill of the nightingale to the saffron hide and dulcet treble of sixty-five." (At this stage his client rose and left the Court.) "The reign of old women has commenced, and if Johanna Southcote converts England to her creed, why should not Ireland, less pious perhaps, kneel before the shrine of the irresistible Widow Wilkins."

Dealing with the claim for damages he said, "Does he claim on the ground of sacrificed affection? Oh! gentlemen, fancy what he has lost—if it were but the blessed raptures of the bridal night! Do not suppose I am going to describe it; I shall leave it to the learned counsel he has selected to compose his epithalamium. I shall not exhibit the venerable trembler—at once a relic and a relict, with a grace for every year and a Cupid in every wrinkle—affecting to shrink from the flame of his impatience and fanning it with the ambrosial sighs of sixty-five! I cannot paint the fierce meridian transports of the honeymoon gradually melting into a more chastened and permanent affection, every nine months adding a link to the chain of their delicate embraces until too soon Death's broadside lays the Lieutenant low consoling, however, his patriarchial charmer (old enough by this time to be the last wife of Methuselah) with a £50 annuity, being the balance of his glory against His Majesty's Ship, Hydra."

He then turned to the plaintiff and his family. "For the gratification of his avarice he was content to embrace age, disease, infirmity and widowhood, to bend his youthful passions to the carcase for which the grave was opening—to feed, by anticipation, on the uncold corpse, and cheat the worm of its reversionary corruption. Educated in a profession proverbially generous, he offered to barter every joy for money! Born in a country ardent to a fault, he advertised his happiness to the highest bidder, and he now solicits an honourable jury to become the panders to this heartless cupidity. Harassed and conspired against, my client entered into the contract you have heard—a contract conceived in meanness, extorted by fraud, and sought to be enforced by the most profligate conspiracy. Trace it through every stage of its progress, in its origin, its means, its effects—from the parent contriving it through the sacrifice of her son and forwarding it through the instrumentality of her daughter, down to the son himself unblushingly acceding to the atrocious combination by which age was to be betrayed and youth degraded, and the odious union of decrepitude and precocious avarice blasphemously consecrated by the solemnities of religion. Gentlemen of the Jury, remember I ask you for no mitigation of damages. Nothing less than your verdict will satisfy me. By that verdict you will sustain the dignity of your sex—by that verdict you will uphold the honour of the national character. I surrender with confidence my case to your decision."

His confidence was not misplaced. Without even retiring the jury, who most of the time had been convulsed with laughter, found for the Defendant, and the Court rose.

The denouément was yet to come. The triumphant Phillips, exulting in his victory, was leaving the Court when he was accosted by his client whose "saffron hide" was now suffused with fury. Armed with a hunting crop she belaboured her brilliant counsel all the way from the courthouse to his lodgings, to the delight of the spectators. At last he was rescued by his learned brethren, and Blake v. Wilkins passed into legal history.

Phillips's subsequent career is not without interest. Had he remained at the Irish Bar there can be no doubt but that he would have attained the highest honours. He soon decided, however, to practise in London where he was an immediate success. The last great case in which he appeared was in the defence of the Swiss valet, Courvoisier, convicted of murdering his master, Lord William Russell. This, incidentally, was one of the first serious crimes investigated by the newly formed Scotland Yard, and it finished Phillips's career as an advocate.

One of the inviolable rules of the Bar is that counsel is not permitted to express to the Court his personal opinion as to the guilt or innocence of his client. His duty begins and ends with presenting the case in its most favourable light, the rest is peculiarly within the province of the jury. This is the case even when he is possessed of no private knowledge. In Courvoisier's case Phillips transgressed this rule in a most aggravated way. Not only did he assert his belief in his client's innocence, in his usual extravagant manner, but it later transpired that Courvoisier had already confessed his guilt to him. This was an impropriety so gross that only the most urgent intervention of influential friends saved him from being disbarred, the condition of lenity being his retiral from practice. The same influence obtained for him the Commissionership for Insolvents in which dull, if lucrative, office he ended his days—a sad anti-climax for an advocate of his brilliance.

It may be observed that he was more fortunate than his compatriot, Doctor Kenneally, whose offence he had anticipated. As a result of his conduct in the prosecution of Orton, the Tichborne Claimant, in which he also expressed his belief in his client's innocence in violent terms, the Doctor was disbarred. Nor was he ever re-admitted, although there was more excuse for him than for his predecessor.

This, then, was the sort of address with which the Irish Courts were regaled, and in which Irish juries revelled, considering no advocate worth listening to who did not employ it. But it was not only juries who were treated to these performances. Frequently Judges, even when sitting alone, found themselves the recipients of counsel's flowery and antithetical periods to which they were perfectly capable of replying in kind. These flights not uncommonly took place in the conduct of the most prosaic proceedings.

For example, motion on affidavit for the transfer of the venue of a civil action would hardly seem an occasion for counsel to exercise his poetic eloquence. Yet such an application to Mr. Justice Ball inspired counsel for the applicant, Frazer, Q.C.

It appears that Mr. Frazer was attempting to have transferred from Galway to Belfast an action for personal injuries, which piece of legal larceny his Lordship was determined to prevent. Having interrupted on several occasions, he inquired, "On what grounds, Mr. Frazer, do you seek to change the venue you have laid in your summons and plaint?"

Mr. Frazer felt grateful to the Court for this further and seasonable interruption, but took the liberty of observing: "I was about to unfold to your lordship the grounds upon which I place my application when your lordship was kind enough to interrupt me for the seventh time. We contend, my lord, that it is the plaintiff's prerogative to lay the venue wherever he chooses. For that proposition I rely on several cases reported in *The Irish Jurist* on that very point, and decided in this very Court, my lord, by two judges who have since died."

Judge Ball again thought fit to intervene. "Who were the judges who made these decisions? Was the Court constituted then as it is now?"

"No, my lord," replied the exasperated but courteous Mr. Frazer, "two of your lordship's brethren, who made these decisions, upon which I rely, have long since left for regions of immortal bliss, where amongst the angelic choirs they sing eternal hallelujahs in a never-ending chorus, which charming society, I trust it will be long before your lordship is called on to join."

At this stage the whole Court shook with laughter, waking up an aged counsel who had gone asleep after a vain attempt to follow the proceedings. The old gentleman inquired what

61

it was all about, to be informed that Frazer had, in effect, told the judge that he wished he had gone to heaven. "Begad! did he say that?" he rejoined. "It is the first bit of sense he has spoken this morning!" Whereupon the ancient began to cough and splutter with laughter himself, so that his brethren were forced to assist him from the Court.

The euphuistic flight of the testy Mr. Frazer, while a little outré, certainly does not stand alone. Every circuit can produce its own stories of kindred passages between Bar and Bench which have added to the gaiety of its records.

In one of these passages, however, the effect was otherwise and it affords a precedent which has not, and can never be, repeated. It took place many years ago in a divisional court of the Exchequer in the course of an address by John Philpot Curran in which he so worked on the emotions of the presiding judge that he was obliged to adjourn the Court.

This remarkable occurrence arose out of a case the circumstances of which were so extraordinary, involving as they did the appearance in the dock of a High Court Judge on a serious criminal charge, that it has become a classic, not merely of legal lore, but of history itself.

In his *Annual Register* for December 10 1803, William Cobbett published a scandalous paper from an anonymous Irish correspondent who signed himself "Juverna". This gentleman had already supplied the editor with a series of virulent attacks on various holders of high office in Dublin, including the Lord Lieutenant, Hardwicke and Mitford, the Lord Chancellor, but that of December—of which William Conyngham Plunkett, the Attorney General, was the target —exceeded in gross defamation anything he had previously written. Attributed to the dock speech of Robert Emmet, whose family and the Plunketts were intimates, it bears repetition. The condemned patriot is purported as referring to Plunkett as: "that viper whom my father nourished! He it was from whose lips I first imbibed those principles and doctrines which now by their effects drag me to the grave: and he it is who is now brought forward as my prosecutor, and

62

who, by an unheard of exercise of the prerogative, has wantonly lashed with a speech the evidence of the dying son of a former friend, when that son had produced no evidence, and made no defence, but, on the contrary, had acknowledged the charge and submitted to his fate."

There was not a word of truth in this diatribe; Emmet had not made even a passing reference to Plunkett who, in fact, had spoken with care and moderation, although the propriety of accepting the brief may be questioned in view of his relationship with the prisoner. At all events, the executive were determined to discover "Juverna", and to that intent Plunkett sued Cobbett and was awarded £500 damages, and the Attorney General, Spencer Perceval (assassinated as Prime Minister in 1812) prosecuted him for seditious libel on the Irish Lord Chancellor.

These proceedings were unquestionably collusive as judgement was never marked, and in the prosecution Cobbett, in abject defiance of the journalists' code, "disclosed his sources" by handing up the written manuscripts which identified "Juverna" beyond peradventure with The Honourable Mr. Justice Robert Johnson, one of His Majesty's Judges of the King's Bench in Ireland.

This put the Government in a quandary, for there was no procedure whereby Johnson could be made amenable on the criminal side in England for libels written in Ireland. Accordingly, Perceval inveighed Parliament into rushing through a Fugitive Offenders Act which enabled English warrants to be executed in Ireland. Ellenborough, the Lord Chief Justice, issued the warrant directing Judge Johnson's arrest. It was backed by an Irish magistrate and the judge was arrested, but before he could be embarked Curran was retained, and the legal battles for his lordship's body began.

The liberty of the subject being involved application could, and can, be made to a judge at any time or place. Curran duly appeared before Chief Justice Downes at his residence to impugn the validity of the warrant in proceedings for habeas corpus. The question being of such moment,

63

Downes invoked the assistance of seven of his brother judges to hear the submissions and the case was argued well into the night, with a neutral result. Of the eight judges, three were in favour of the legality of the warrant, three against it, and two refused to express an opinion. The Chief Justice referred the matter to the decision of a divisional court of the King's Bench, which decided by a majority of two judges to one against Curran's contention.

In a question of this nature the citizen is entitled to pursue his remedy from judge to judge and court to court, and Curran caused a fresh writ of *habeas corpus* to issue in the Court of Exchequer, presided over by the Lord Chief Baron Barry Yelverton, Earl of Avonmore. In order to appreciate what follows it is necessary to understand the relationship between judge and counsel.

Yelverton was a man of the deepest culture, probably the very first classicist of his day, and for many years Curran had been accustomed to spend his most enjoyable hours with him as an intimate guest in his home. Together they started the St. Patrick's Society, better known as the Monks of the Screw, of which Yelverton was founder, and Curran first prior—incidentally, Johnson was sacristan. Although a convivial association, this was no mere drinking club and included among its very jealously selected members were the choicest spirits of the day, as such names as Grattan, Ponsonby and Charlemont testify.

Among them the art of conversation achieved a distinction which has never since been approached, even in a city famous for that accomplishment. Unfortunately, it was all too good to last, and as a result of one of those ridiculous quarrels which merely scratch the surface of acquaintance-ship, but can disrupt the firmest friendship, Curran and Yelverton fell out and for years ceased to recognize each other. The club itself disbanded and it was in the incongruous surroundings of a court of law that sacristan, prior and founder met each other yet again, but in the strange capacities of prisoner, counsel and judge.

Curran with his accustomed ability had argued in the King's Bench that the warrant was bad as the Act under which had been issued related only to an offender who had fled the jurisdiction. In the Exchequer he had at some length presented the same submissions with cogency but formality. At last, however, when he came to criticize the reasoning of the King's Bench, his feelings of affection for his old friend became so revived that quite spontaneously he was impelled to continue. "I am not ignorant that this extraordinary construction has received the sanction of another court, nor of the surprise and dismay with which it smote upon the general heart of the Bar. I am aware that I may have the mortification of being told in another country of that unhappy decision, and I foresee in what confusion I shall hang down my head when I am told it. But I cherish too the consolatory hope that I shall be able to tell them that I had an old and learned friend, whom I would put above all the sweepings of their hall, who was of a different opinion [a delicate reference to Ellenborough and Perceval] who had derived his ideas of civil liberty from the purest fountains of Athens and Rome; who had fed the youthful vigour of his studious mind with the theoretic knowledge of their wisest philosophers and statesmen; and who had refined the theory into the quick and exquisite sensibility of moral instinct by contemplating the practice of their illustrious examples— by dwelling on the sweet-souled piety of Cimon, on the anticipated Christianity of Socrates, on the gallant and pathetic patriotism of Epaminondas, on that pure austerity of Fabricius whom to move from his integrity would have been more difficult than to have pushed the sun from its course.

"I would add, that if he seemed to hesitate, it was but for a moment; that his hesitation was like a passing cloud that floats across the morning sun and hides it from the view, and does so for a moment hide it, without even approaching the face of the luminary. And this soothing hope I draw from the dearest and tenderest recollections of my life—from the remembrance of those Attic nights and those reflections of the gods which we have partaken with those admired, and respected, and beloved companions who have gone before us, over whose ashes the most precious tears of Ireland have been shed." (At this recollection, Avonmore became so affected that he put his head in his hands, and wept himself.)

Curran continued: "Yes, my good lord, I see you do not forget them; I see their sacred forms passing in sad review before your memory; I see your pained and softened fancy recalling those happy meetings, when the innocent enjoyment of social mirth expanded into the nobler warmth of social virtue, and the horizon of the board became expanded into the horizon of man; when the swelling heart conceived and communicated the pure and generous purpose, when my slenderer and young taper imbibed its borrowed light from the more matured and redundant fountain of yours. Yes, my lord, we can remember those nights, without any other regret than they can never more return; for

'We spent them not in toys, or lust, or wine,
But search of deep philosophy,
Wit, eloquence, and poesy—
Arts which I loved, for they, my friend, were thine.' "

This sustained and touching tribute is without parallel, and its grace and poignant evocations so overcame his lordship that one of the junior judges announced that they would rise for a short respite.

During this interval Avonmore sent for Curran to come to his chambers where at last the two old friends effected their reconciliation, the need for which should never have arisen.

It speaks well for the even-handed justice dispensed by the Chief Baron, that on the resumption, although he said that he had difficulty in disengaging his feelings from the effects of that fascinating eloquence which still acted on his heart, he voted with the majority of his judicial brethren in favour of the legality of Johnson's arrest.

The indefatigable Curran then brought one last application to the Common Pleas, and yet again was defeated by a majority. He had now run out of judges and his client was brought to London whereupon at his trial he was found guilty of seditious libel. Johnson, however, was indestructible. The English executive were by now heartily sick of the hornet's nest they had stirred up for themselves in Ireland, and during the Judge's summing up they directed the prosecution team to withdraw from the Court. Sentence was then deferred until the following term. It was never carried out because the Government in the meantime resigned, and the party of Charles James Fox assumed office.

Fox rightly felt that the Fugitive Offenders Act had been a fraud on the House. Accordingly, the ineffable Mr. Justice Johnson who, however illegal and disgraceful his arrest, was an unmitigated and defamatory liar, was allowed to retire from his judgeship on a pension to the amount of his full salary. He displayed his gratitude by transferring himself to Paris where he engaged himself in bombarding Napoleon with plans for the destruction of the British fleet and the overthrow of that Government from which he derived a not illiberal income. There we may leave him, for there he died.

It is difficult to over-emphasize the effect of great oratory on the Irish, and while one can well understand the appeal to any audience inherent in such persuasive eloquence as Curran's, it is hard to credit that such was the regard of an Irishman for an able speech that even the prisoner on a capital charge could express his unfeigned appreciation of an address by prosecuting counsel that was designed to bring him to the gallows. And yet no less an authority than Sir John Ross, the last Lord Chancellor of Ireland, was present at a trial in which that very thing happened.

A professional assassin who was reputed to have murdered more than thirty people had been hired by a bloodthirsty old farmer to shoot his son-in-law, which was done with a revolver. To implicate the old ruffian the expert forced

67

him to empty the remaining chambers into the body. This so worked on the old man's mind that, horror-stricken, he confessed and was convicted and hanged; but the jury disagreed twice in regard to the actual perpetrator as his accomplice's statements were inadmissible in evidence against him.

On the third trial Serjeant, later Lord, Hemphill made a powerful speech which quite clearly excited the admiration of the prisoner. When counsel sat down he turned to the warder, who was standing beside him in the dock, and said enthusiastically: "I don't give a damn what anyone says, that's the best bloody speech ever, and that bit about the innocent blood calling from the earth was the best of all. Be God, I never heard the oul' Serjeant so good; I didn't think he had it in him!"

# 5

# *Good Men and True*

From the professional side of the Law one turns naturally to a consideration of the lay branch of its administration in the Courts, the Jury System. Unknown to the code of the native Irish, it is of peculiarly English origin. In its Irish manifestation it has been variously described as "the last great buttress of civil liberty", and "a mockery, a delusion and a snare". Oddly enough, a strong case can be made for either proposition, because the vagaries of Irish jurymen are as unpredictable as the way of the biblical ship in the midst of the sea.

Nor is this capriciousness altogether surprising when it is appreciated that considerable ingenuity and imagination has been exercised by the executive to ensure that liability for jury service should fall only on that part of the community least able to support it, and least qualified to discharge it. To these intents, Authority in its inscrutable wisdom exempts, in fact prohibits, from jury service anyone remotely connected with the law, and who might be expected to understand and weigh the evidence; in this forbidden category are also included most of the learned professions. Above all, the civil servants, who represent by far the widest stratum among the leisured classes, are exempt on the theory that the daily discharge of their duties is so vital to the public weal that not even one of them can be spared for the furtherance of justice. On the other hand, the small shopkeeper, or commercial traveller, who finds himself on a jury in a murder trial lasting three weeks, will not infrequently find his concentration on the evidence somewhat distracted by the contemplation of the financial havoc being wreaked on his private affairs.

Perhaps the most noteworthy feature of the system is the fact that other than being a rated occupier of premises of a minimum and modest valuation, in order to be enrolled on the panel absolutely no other qualification is demanded. In this regard the framer of the laws is distinguished from his fellow who helps to administer them. Whereas the former requires no property qualification whatsoever, he must be able to sign his name before taking his seat in the House, no such oppressive test of literacy is imposed on the citizen before taking his in the jury-box. All that is required is that he be over twenty-one and under sixty-five, able to draw breath, and not manifestly insane.

This remarkable institution was introduced into Ireland in a primitive form by the invading Norman kings, and we find the first mention of its being in operation in that small area around Dublin, which represented the possessions of Henry III, called the Pale. At this time, however, in England the institution had already been developing for centuries, and its origins are lost in the mists of Anglo-Saxon antiquity. Originally, a man accused of a crime could call on a number of men from his "hundred" who, if they asserted their belief in his innocence, on their oath, would obtain his acquittal. This was known as compurgation, and the gentlemen who concurrently chanted their testimony in chorus, as compurgators, or consacramentales, by reason of the sacred nature of the oath.

The first reference to this singular procedure is in an ordinance of King Alfred, who was a better law reformer than a baker, which prescribed: "If a King's thane be accused of manslaying, and if he dare to clear himself, let him do so with twelve King's thanes."

It must not be supposed, however, that the magic number, twelve, was the standard; depending on the type of offence it varied from as few as six to as many as thirty-five, a tall order indeed.

After the Conquest, the Normans adopted and adapted the compurgation of the Anglo-Saxons which ultimately became refined, if that is the word, into something approaching the Jury system as we know it to-day. At the same time they brought in their own exotic and bloodthirsty forms of trial, which coexisted with the older system, and became part of the common law, in some cases for seven hundred and fifty years.

The most usual and typical of these was Trial by Battel (not battle, as it is commonly and erroneously spelled). The proceeding was known as an Appeal of Battel (from the French *appeller*), and arose after an accusation had been preferred and a defence stated. Both the charge of the appeller, or accuser, and the defence of the accused were required to be set out with precision, the least defect in either being fatal to the interests of the erring party. If the defence was a denial, Glanville informs us, the issue was then directed to be resolved in a single combat. The accused might decline this enlightened method of asserting his innocence if he were over sixty, or maimed, in which event he was obliged to undergo the ordeal of hot iron if he were a freeman, or hot water if a villein; if he failed the test by ordeal he was, of course, hanged. In the circumstances it is not to be wondered at that age or infirmity was rarely pleaded.

On the actual trial, the parties appeared each armed with a stave and light shield, no other weapon or protection being allowed. If the accused fought until the stars appeared or killed his adversary, he was acquitted; if he were overcome, he was hanged. If the accuser survived, but lost the fight, he, in turn, was liable to punishment at the King's pleasure.

The duel was also a popular mode for the trial of civil disputes, particularly for the determination of knotty questions of title to land, and defendants in actions for debt often found it a most expedient and satisfactory way of resolving their difficulties. Indeed one can readily visualize considerable public support for a private member's bill for the revival of this form of defence, although it would probably meet with some opposition from such vested interests as hire-purchase companies and income tax collectors.

Perilous as it was to be owed money by a lusty debtor, by far the most dangerous characters to have any truck with in mediaeval times were the women, and in particular, as ever, with widows. A woman could bring an appeal of battel, naming her champion, for personal injuries, and a widow for the death of her husband. If the unfortunate accused denied the charge he underwent the ordeal which, from his point of view, constituted an admirable example of the principle of "heads you win, tails I lose", and created an occupational male risk which probably accounts to some extent for the popularity of the monastic way of life in those days.

It is satisfactory to record in parenthesis, that the female did not have it all her own way. A spinster who lived alone, especially if she were foolhardy enough to own a cat, was liable on any, or no, provocation to be suspected of being a witch. This suspicion usually entailed most uncomfortable consequences, the least of which was the water ordeal. This mode of proof involved the ceremonious dumping of the suspect into a pond. On the plausible theory that the pure element would reject the corrupt and welcome the virtuous, if the lady floated she was guilty, if she sank, innocent. In the first case she was burned to death, in the second merely drowned.

It remains to add that trial by battel, on both the civil and criminal sides, was abolished by statute only as recently as 1819, as a result of a murder case the previous year. This was the famous case of Ashford v. Thornton, in which a young girl called Mary Ashford was murdered in circumstances of peculiar savagery. The evidence pointed overwhelmingly to the guilt of an Abraham Thornton, and the victim's brother instituted a prosecution for murder against him. Thornton, who was a powerful and dangerous brute, insisted on his right to wager a battel, and his accuser's advisers prevailed on him not to appear, but to allow the law to take its course in the courts. Thornton was accordingly indicted for murder at the next sessions when he successfully pleaded *autrefois acquit*, and a reluctant judge was compelled to discharge him.

This flagrant miscarriage of justice spelled the end of battel as a mode of trial, and thereafter prisoners on serious charges must entrust their liberty to the, perhaps, equally hazardous, if more sedate, determination of their peers in the jury box.

All these procedural niceties were foreign to the Irish until they were imported by the invaders into the corpus of the Law. The original inhabitants of the island had their own indigenous code which in pre-Christian times was expounded by the Druids. Unfortunately, the law reports of the decisions of these functionaries are not available, if they ever existed. If we are to judge by the proceedings adopted by their royal Celtic masters, to whom they were advisers, we may conclude that their jurisprudence was no less ferocious than that of the Anglo-Saxon or the Norman. For instance, in one period we read of eight kings each gaining the throne by murdering his predecessor, and a little later, of thirteen monarchs in succession meeting violent deaths. Connla the Comely appropriately died in bed, in which he was more fortunate than his four successors. Then came Rory the Great who had a peaceful passing, but each of his successors was slaughtered.

The Druids were magicians as well as judges, and their magic seems to have been pretty powerful if the unforeseeable catastrophes which befell such monarchs as survived the perils of battle and assassination are any indication. Even the direful King Daithe who, when he had exterminated most of his Irish colleagues, decided to visit the Continent and exterminate a few Teutonic monarchs as a change, was struck by lightning at the foot of the Alps—an occurrence reliably attributed to Druidical intervention. This, however, was their last spectacular coup, soon Saint Patrick arrived, and that was the end of Druidism.

From the successful and peaceful progress of the good Saint in the accomplishment of his mission amid such as turbulent people, it is not unreasonable to conclude that the charms of their sorcerous lawgivers were beginning to pall on the Irish. Henceforward, Irish jurisprudence was purged of paganism and the code of the Brehon Law was established throughout the land. The more farseeing of the Druids bowed to the inevitable, and in anticipation of the golden rule of the American General, "if you can't lick 'em, join 'em", embraced the new order and became Brehons themselves.

The concept of the separation of the powers of the executive and the judiciary was unknown to the Irish, and the Brehons acted both as Ministers of State and Judges. If they were men of peace, their masters certainly ignored their ministerial advice, because the Irish scene continued to be one of battles, massacres, burnings and pillage. Even when the Scandinavian hordes arrived, the native rulers, with fine impartiality, sometimes fought them, but as frequently joined forces with them the better to plunder their neighbours.

As judges, however, their prestige was high and their courts were accorded both respect and obedience. Their decisions were equitable and, although they were laymen, ecclesiastics submitted to them in matters not purely canonical. Indeed, the best proof of the justice of the Brehon code lies in the fact that it governed the lives of the Irish people, except in a few small areas, until it was finally extinguished in the seventeenth century.

The beginning of that century marked the end of the Gaelic civilization. Up to that time there had never really been a conquest except in the area of the Pale. The Normans and English, it is well to remember, originally came over at the invitation of the Irish to help them in their domestic quarrels; they had adopted the native customs and language, intermarried with their great families, and eventually became more Irish than the Irish themselves. Until the Battle of Kinsale it had been warfare, but with the Flight of the Earls in 1607 the last unifying leaven of Celtic society was lost for ever, and thenceforward it was rebellion.

Now also began that gradual revolution which it was the set policy of the Crown to effect. The immemorial usages of religion, custom and even costume were proscribed. The lands of the Irish and Anglo-Irish aristocracy were expropriated and allotted among the monarch's catamites, his lowland Scotch compatriots, and a society of adventurers of the City of London. Over vast areas there was a solitude, but none could call it peace. In the words of Donald O'Neill, quoted by the French historian, Thierry, "Hatred produced by lengthened recollections of injustice, by the murder of our fathers, brothers, and kindred, will not be extinguished in our time, nor in that of our sons."

The most important step in the process of Anglicization was the superseding of the Brehon by the English law, and with the disappearance of the distinction between the Pale and the rest of the country the latter code became, in theory at least, the law of Ireland. Under its embracing protection, it was asserted, all Irishmen were entitled equally with their English brethren to the enjoyment of its rights and privileges. Very soon, however, it was brought home to the natives with no uncertain force that this pious principle did not obtain in practice, and that the very forms and procedure of the new dispensation could be employed to despoil and victimize them.

From this misguided policy there stemmed that historic antipathy to the English regime which down the years has had such incalculable and unfortunate repercussions. It is a paradox of legal history that at the very time when Coke and

75

Bacon were laying the foundations of modern English jurisprudence there was being created among the Irish of every
class a tradition, which became instinctive, that Justice could
only be obtained by them through a wary and suspicious
approach from windward of the Law.

The recipients of the first blast of the wind of change,
which the new procedure of trial by jury generated, were the
proprietors of the ancient lands of Connaught. It blew away
their titles, their rights and their wealth at the behest of Sir
Thomas, Lord Wentworth, Lord Deputy of Ireland, who
was rewarded by his royal master Charles I, with the Earldom
of Strafford, and later the headman's axe in the Tower of
London.

Of James I it can at least be said that he did not attempt
to attach the colour of any right, other than that of conquest, to his expropriation of the lands of Ulster. The martyr
king, however, in a pretended regard for the forms of legality,
through Wentworth (that "great bad man") proceeded to
perpetrate "injustice under the guise of justice—robbery
under the revered forms of law." To this intent, special commissions were directed under which the Commissioners were
empowered to empanel juries to inquire into the titles under
which the whole territory of Connaught, consisting of Leitrim, Roscommon, Sligo, Mayo, the County of Galway and
the County of the town of Galway, were held. Juries were
sworn to try "what estate, right or title the King, or any of his
progenitors, had, or of right *ought to have had*, to the whole
territory" of each county.

The attendance of the Lord Deputy on the bench in every
trial was made even more formidable by the presence of an
array of soldiery drawn up in ranks of horse, gun and foot.
Backed up by the most specious arguments, the Attorney
General informed the jurors that it was his Majesty's intention to make them a rich and civil people and participators
in the glorious work of reformation which he had under-
taken. Nor were promises lacking that the jurors themselves

76

would not be forgotten in the redistribution of the land, an inducement that was held out to the judges themselves. In fact Lowther, Chief Justice of the Common Pleas, was given twenty per cent of the first year's rent raised by the Commis-sioners. Thus cajoled and threatened, the juries surrendered their consciences to their terror, and in Leitrim, Roscommon, Sligo and Mayo found in favour of the meretricious pretensions of the Crown.

In Galway, however, to their undying honour, the jury refused indignantly to sanctify robbery with the halo of legality, and unanimously found against the Crown.

The upshot was spectacular, and forcibly brought home to the Irish what trial by their peers entailed when the verdict offended the interests of the Government. The inquisition took place on August 14 1635 in Portumna Castle, and the Lord Deputy was as usual on the bench. Transported with fury, he had all the jurors instantly arrested and consigned to the dungeons, whence they were conveyed in chains to the hardly more salubrious confines of Dublin Castle. There they were put on trial before Sir Gerard Lowther, of the twenty per cent, and were each fined £4,000, a vast sum in those days. Their estates were seized and themselves sentenced to be imprisoned until their fines were paid. Their petition to be discharged was refused, except on condition of making a public acknowledgement not merely of an error of judgement, but of actual perjury in their verdict—terms which they contemptuously disdained. The High Sheriff of Galway, Martin D'Arcy, who had convened the jury, fared even worse. His estates were also escheated, and he was thrown into prison where he was tortured to death.

Wentworth sent a detailed account of these proceedings to Mr. Secretary Coke at Whitehall who received it with high approbation and wrote that "it gave great satisfaction to his Majesty and all those who attended him in this business". The minister continued his letter in these terms: "The scarcity of Protestants and the plenty of priests and Jesuits in Galway is very considerable, and which may be reformed;

and such counsellors-at-law as have so forwardly and maliciously opposed the King's title, are justly to be pressed, either to take the oath of supremacy or to be suspended from their practice as not fit men to profess the law for others which themselves will not obey." It concludes, "A greater proportion of the land should be taken from the pretended owners in the County of Galway than in the rest of the province."

Two years passed before effect was given to this last adjuration but finally, in St. Francis's Abbey, the county jury, and in the Tholsel Hall the jury for the county of the town, found in favour of the King's title. Their verdicts, however cowardly, were hardly surprising, as many of their persecuted predecessors of the Portumna Castle trial were by now either dead or dying in prison, whereas the juries of the other counties had been extravagantly rewarded. Likewise counsel for the Crown had been promoted, and the advocates for justice degraded and disbarred.

History records these proceedings as the Strafford Inquisitions. Their immediate effect was to populate the province with strangers and depopulate it of its rightful owners, of whom one half in Galway, and one quarter in the other counties, were dispossessed. But the ultimate results were even more far-reaching. As this was the introduction to the Irish of the jury system, it set the headline. It also struck a note of cynical perversity that sounded down the administration of the law for more than two and a half centuries, the echoes of which have not yet died out. In Ireland thenceforward, where political or other governmental interests were involved in legal trials, a systematic course of jury-packing and corruption became conventional, and the verdicts of the bodies so selected were fore-ordained before a word of evidence had been heard.

It should also be said that in ordinary criminal and civil cases where the prerogatives of the State were not engaged the jury was usually impartially empanelled. This however, did not ensure disinterested verdicts. The disregard by authority when it was expedient, for the spirit, and indeed the letter, of justice, bred in turn a corresponding attitude in the people, which often produced the most startling tragic, and hilarious results.

Well indeed might Lord Justice Denman, as late as the middle of the last century, characterize trial by jury in Ireland as "a mockery, a delusion, and a snare".

It may be added that a few typical examples of the operation of the system in Ireland will establish that his lordship's assessment rested on a more solid foundation than the desire to deliver a well-turned aphorism.

# 6

# Trial by their Peers

The trial of Nicholas Sheehy for the murder of John Bridge is perhaps unique. At the same time it contains so many features of cynical disregard for the due process of law as to distinguish it as an archetype of what was to become almost conventional in the operation of the jury system.

The unfortunate Sheehy was the Catholic parish priest of Clogheen in the County Tipperary. Because of the Penal Laws, he had been educated in France before returning to Ireland, a circumstance which in itself did not endear him to the Francophobe feelings of the upper classes of the time. He was of a gentle and saintly disposition, and was wont impartially to condemn the outrages of both Orange landlordism and Whiteboyism. As a result he incurred the deadly enmity of those inveterate elements among the landowners from whom the magistracy was selected.

Whiteboyism was the crystallization of that agrarian and religious bitterness into which the laws had provoked the peasantry, the mass of the population. The Whiteboys were so called because, like their imitators the Ku Klux Klan, they ranged abroad at night disguised in white sheets. Like so many agrarian gangs which succeeded them, they were oath-bound and the most daring and ruthless of the small farmers and labourers were members. They also included in their ranks, apart from those with a sense of injustice, blackguards of all descriptions from murderers to arsonists, and above all, informers. The vengence of such men, even the best of them, driven as they were to desperation by the exactions of their landlords, and especially of the tithe-proctors, was terrible and often indiscriminate. To such a state of panic did it re-duce the Government that a succession of enactments for the suppression of unlawful societies was passed, and even to be found "affording comfort and aid" to a Whiteboy was in itself a serious offence, while to be a member was treason.

In spite of every effort at suppression Whiteboyism under one guise or another was rampant. The reason was to be found in that terrible penal code of law which was described by Samuel Johnson as "more grevious than the ten pagan persecutions of the Christians", and by Edmund Burke as "a machine of wise and deliberate contrivance, as well fitted for the oppression, impoverishment, and degradation of a people, and the debasement in them of human nature itself, as ever proceeded from the perverted ingenuity of man."

These were the legal and social conditions which prevailed in the country, and most conspicuously in the county of Tipperary when early in the year 1765 a semi-imbecile vagrant called John Bridge included the town of Clonmel in his wandering itinerary. In the course of soliciting drinks from the habitués of the lower taverns of the town, the simple-minded Bridge was ill advised enough to boast freely that very soon he would have plenty of money to spend as he was going to give paid evidence against various people, whom he was foolish enough to name, as being Whiteboys, at the next Sessions. As Bridge was precisely the type of individual who was employed as a professional informer, these an-nouncements bore the hallmark of truth. In the circumstances, it is hardly surprising that he failed to turn up to give his evidence at the Assizes, with the result that a large number of prosecutions had to be abandoned.

This anti-climax infuriated the extremists among the gentry who determined upon a scapegoat. Accordingly, a clergyman called Hewison, who was particularly diligent in tithe collecting and correspondingly frightened, induced three informers to swear informations against Father Nicholas Sheehy. These three informants were one Mary Dunlea, better known in Clonmel as "Moll the Whore", a horse-thief called Toohey, who was pardoned for his assistance to the authorities, and a tinker called Lanigan. The informations of this trio set out (a) that they, and each of them had seen Father Sheehy administering the Whiteboy oath, and (b) that he was present at, and assisted in, the murder of John Bridge.

Despite the characters of his accusers and the absurdity of the charges, the priest knew he was in mortal danger and immediately went into hiding, whereupon a reward of £300 was proclaimed for his apprehension. A friendly landlord took him under his protection, and after many months eventually persuaded his guest to surrender to the authorities in Dublin where his innocence would be speedily established. The advice was taken and Father Sheehy offered to surrender on condition that he not be tried in Clonmel "where the nature of my enemies is stronger than their love of justice". This condition was accepted, and on February 10, 1766 he stood his trial before the Court of the King's Bench presided over by the Chief Justice.

The case did not last long. The alleged evidence for the Crown was treated with contempt by the Court, and the accused's innocence was so manifest that in directing an acquittal the Chief Justice referred in the strongest terms to the magistracy who had prosecuted an accusation which was nothing less than an abuse of the process of justice, and went on to say that he would have pleasure in seeing it in the dock in place of its present occupant.

The prisoner was duly discharged but immediately an appalling thing happened. His liberty lasted less than a minute because his Tipperary persecutors, undaunted by the Chief Justice's strictures, had him re-arrested on the charge of complicity in Bridge's murder. Over this course the King's Bench had no jurisdiction and the unfortunate cleric was shackled, flung into an open cart, and in that way conveyed to Clonmel under armed escort and for three days exposed to the elements.

The prosecution ensured that there be no possibility of escape for Father Sheehy by entrusting the selection of the jury into the capable hands of the sheriff, Daniel Toler, whose son, as Lord Norbury, was to add further lustre to the family name.

The trial itself which came off on March 12 at Clonmel was a tragic farce. The same evidence which had been scari-fied in the King's Bench was this time received with appro-bation. Several of the defence witnesses, including the accused's brother who could prove an unshakable alibi, had been indicted themselves and thus rendered incompetent to give evidence. In spite of this, the accused was able to call the mother of "Moll the Whore" who swore that her daughter had never left their cottage on the night of the alleged murder. Further, a prominent Protestant landowner called Keating informed the Court that Father Sheehy had slept that night in his, Keating's, house and could not possibly have been present at the time. For his pains, and at the in-stance of the ineffable Hewison, Keating was himself arrested on a fictitious charge of the murder of a sergeant and cor-poral on the occasion of a rescue of some Whiteboys, and dragged off in chains to Kilkenny gaol. There he was in due course tried and acquitted, the Judge saying that "there was not the vestige of a foundation for the charge".

Father Sheehy was less fortunate. The fact that Bridge's corpse was never found, and indeed that there was evidence that he was alive and well in Limerick, weighed not at all with the jury. This body was entirely composed of vindictive men determined to have Father Sheehy's life and they found him Guilty, despite the judge's charge which was favourable to an acquittal.

The verdict was signalized by a dramatic incident, when the attorney for the accused shouted that they were shedding the blood of an innocent man, and that God would wreak vengeance on those responsible. For this protest he had to flee the county.

Father Sheehy was duly hanged amid scenes of unprecedented uproar. On the scaffold he forgave his enemies, but the enraged and riotous thousands who were present did not and it took a battalion of dragoons to disperse them.

The attorney proved to have been a remarkable prophet. Every single one of the jury died violently and atrociously, two by committing suicide in fits of insane remorse, and within two generations not a descendant of theirs was to be found in the county. Of the three perjured witnesses, "Moll the Whore" shortly afterwards fell to her death in a Cork brothel. She was luckier than her colleagues for Toohey, the horse thief, died in lingering agony from syphilis, and Lanigan, the tinker, from leprosy.

This dreadful trial had the most incalculable effect on the people. More than any other case it was responsible for the utter disrepute and hatred in which the jury system came to be regarded by the vast majority of the Irish, who looked upon it as yet another deadly weapon in the hands of their oppressors.

A further and, as events were to show, not unimportant effect which the martyrdom of Nicholas Sheehy had was to determine a young student's future. This was John Philpot Curran who, it is said, was so affected by the case as to decide on a career at the Bar. In his turn he was to have a wide experience of the perfidy of Irish juries.

The case in which this quality was most notably displayed was in the prosecution of William Orr at the Bloody Assizes held in the Trinity term at Carrickfergus in 1797. In these assizes the law achieved a new level of ferocity, only to be surpassed in the events of the following year. William Orr was a Presbyterian farmer, thirty-one years of age, married with five young children, and of the highest repute among his neighbours. Although defended by Curran, he was wrongfully convicted in circumstances so flagitious as to be almost incredible.

Later in the year Peter Finnerty, Editor of the Dublin Press, was indicted for criminal libel for publishing an open letter to Camden, the Lord Lieutenant, in which, among other home truths, the following passage occurs:

"The death of Mr. Orr, the nation has pronounced one of the most sanguinary and savage acts that had disgraced the laws. In perjury, did you not hear, my Lord, the verdict was given? Perjury accompanied with terror, as terror has marked every step of your government. Vengeance and desolation were to fall on those who would not plunge themselves in blood. These were not strong enough; against the express law of the land, not only was drink introduced to the jury, but drunkenness itself, beastly and criminal drunkenness, was employed to procure the murder of a better man than any that now surrounds you.

"Stung with remorse, in the return of reason, part of the jury solemnly and soberly made oath that their verdict had been given under the unhappy influence of intimidation and drink, and in the most serious affidavit that ever was made, by acknowledging their crime, endeavoured to atone to God and to their country for the sin into which they had been seduced. And though the innocence of the accused remained doubtful it was your duty, my Lord, to have interposed your arm and saved him from the death that perjury, drunkenness and reward had prepared for him. Innocent it appears he was; his blood has been shed, and the precedent indeed is awful."

Commenting on this passage in his defence of Finnerty, Curran had this to say:

"William Orr was indicted for having administered the oath of a United Irishman. Every man now knows what that oath is; that it is simply an engagement first, to promote a brotherhood of affection among men of all religious distinctions; secondly, to labour for the attainment of a parliamentary reform; and thirdly, an obligation of secrecy, which was added to it when the Convention Law made it criminal and punishable to meet by any public delegation for that purpose. After remaining upwards of a year in gaol, Mr. Orr was brought to his trial; was prosecuted by the

State; was sworn against by a common informer of the name of Wheatley, who himself had taken the obligation, and was convicted under the Insurrection Act, which makes the administering such an obligation felony of death. . . . Three of the jurors made solemn affidavit in court that liquor had been conveyed into their room; that they were brutally threatened by some of their fellow jurors with capital punishment if they did not find the prisoner guilty, and that worn down by watching and intoxication, they had given a verdict of guilty against him, although they believed him in their consciences to be innocent. That further enquiries were made, which ended in a discovery of the infamous life and bad character of the informer: that a respite was therefore sent once, twice and thrice, to give time, as Mr. Attorney General had stated, for his Excellency to consider whether mercy could be extended to him or not; and that, with a knowledge of all these circumstances, his Excellency did finally determine that mercy should not be extended to him; and that he was accordingly executed upon that verdict."

Shocking as these circumstances appear, Curran had spoken with a moderation designed to persuade a jury biased against his client, Finnerty. The real facts were even worse than those he had detailed to that tribunal. He did not tell them that the information against Orr was sworn to satisfy a private enmity by George Macartney, vicar of Antrim, who hated Presbyterians even more than Papists, a gentleman whom the High Sheriff, Lord Massarene, not over scrupulous himself, had designated as "not of Christ, but of Satan"; nor that one of the prosecution counsel was Macartney's nephew. Apart from the infamous character of the informer Wheatley, it had emerged that two witnesses for the Crown had received £100 each in return for perjured evidence. The jurors' affidavits had disclosed that, locked up as they were for eleven hours, they were vomiting from drink, and that the oldest had been threatened with being thrown out of the window if he maintained his attitude in favour of an acquittal.

As in Sheehy's case, the soldiers surrounded the scaffold on the morning of the execution. At the last moment before the drumbeat the prisoner shouted, "Remember Orr."

In his peroration in Finnerty's case, which was in reality

a trial to vindicate the memory of William Orr, Curran enjoined the Green Street jury, "Let me, therefore, remind you
that, though the day may soon come when our ashes shall be
scattered before the winds of heaven, the memory of what
you do cannot die; it will carry down to your posterity your
honour, or your shame."

The jury convicted Finnerty, and the people remembered
Orr.

The effects of such cases were so to disease the attitude
of both the governed and the governing towards the administration of justice in Ireland that even to-day the infection has
not been eradicated. The great historian, Lecky, in an immortal passage in which he surveys the Irish legal scene in
the nineteenth century, says:

"In England, with the rarest exceptions, public opinion in all
classes is on the side of the law, and all classes desire the detec-
tion, conviction, and punishment of criminals. In Ireland great
departments of crime are thoroughly organised; looked upon as
of the nature of war; supported by the whole force of popular
opinion; screened from punishment by the most deliberate perjury or the most savage and systematic intimidation of witnesses.
The frequent impossibility of obtaining convictions in a disturbed
county for certain classes of crime in spite of the clearest evidence; the extreme difficulty of obtaining evidence even when
crimes are committed in open daylight and to the knowledge of
numbers; the numerous cases of the murder of witnesses, or even
of the families of witnesses; the great sums which Governments
have been compelled to pay in order to transport honest witnesses
or their families beyond the range of popular vengeance, are all
signs of a diseased community in which the normal methods of
administering justice often fail to work. It has in consequence
been found necessary to combat crime by far more stringent
measures than would be required in England. Suspensions of the
Habeas Corpus Act, Insurrection Acts of great severity, frequent
change of venue, and careful selection of jurymen have all been
necessary. Not only prosecuting counsel, but even judges, have
constantly adopted a tone, in enforcing the guilt of criminals
upon juries, which would hardly have been tolerated in England;
and in the absence through fear or sympathy of more respectable
witnesses, paid informers, often of the most disreputable character, and criminals seeking as King's evidence to escape punishment, have played a great part. Even in ordinary cases the Irish

witness, with his cunning, his dexterity of fence, his dislike to simple and straightforward answers, his picturesque, diffuse, evasive phraseology, often gives an Irish trial an appearance which is very strange to an English eye; and to all this we must add the intense political and religious passion that has been constantly imported into Irish courts, and the power which appeal to such passions has often had upon witnesses and juries."

From this passage it can be seen that the dice were not always loaded in favour of the Crown. Even the most carefully empanelled jury cannot find a verdict of Guilty if there is no evidence to go before it. For that matter, later on in the last century when the right and liability to serve on juries was extended to all but the most insignificant property holders, even the most obviously guilty criminal was accorded the benefit of the jury's antipathy to the Establishment. For this reason jury selection in Ireland called forth from the law officers and officials a high and effective artistry, so much so that Lord Chief Justice O'Brien, who sat well into the twentieth century, was, and is, never referred to as other than "Pether the Packer", a simple tribute to his powers of ingenuity.

All in all, if the indictment charged a non-political crime, as for instance larceny, rape or arson, the verdict of the unpacked jury might or might not—probably not—be honest. If, on the other hand, it charged sedition, or some other offence obnoxious to the prerogatives of authority, then an unwritten rule, as inexorable as the law of the Medes and the Persians, was invoked. The jury was packed, and packed so scientifically as to make trial a formality and conviction a certainty.

The plight of a juryman in Ireland was certainly unenviable. On the one hand he was liable to the disfavour of the Crown, and on the other to the contempt, if no worse, of his neighbours. Probably only in the comparative anonymity of a city as large as Dublin could he feel reasonably immune from the consequences of his verdict. Certainly only in Dublin was there a likelihood of that verdict being impartial—political cases, of course, always excepted.

Another hazard they had to face was that of the presiding judge who, not infrequently playing on their ignorance of their rights, bullied and frightened them into a finding of fact which should have been peculiarly within their own province. For example, some of the charges of Norbury, which have come down to us, to recalcitrant juries are hair-raising, even though we know that the judge lacked the power to enforce his threats. His auditors regarded the power of the Bench as all-embracing, and in playing on this mis-apprehension his lordship set a standard which was to be followed by his successors for many years.

On the question of recalcitrance not every judicial threat was an idle one. There were, until the gradual reform of the system, various powers for bringing a jury to heel which were perfectly legal. For instance, in a criminal trial the rule was that they were to be locked up incommunicado and deprived of food and drink until they reached a verdict. One would have thought that this wise provision should have been suffi-cient to ensure a definite result, but the law had yet another pitfall for the indecisive. This was known as the procedure of Carting of Juries to the verge of the county, and having regard to the weather in Ireland and the condition of the roads one can well imagine that it proved a fairly coercive inducement to come to a decision.

The operation of the system is well exemplified in the case of The King v. McDiarmad which is notable for no other juristic reason than that this procedure for once failed to achieve its purpose.

The accused, a professional burglar by occupation, was indicted at the Roscommon Assizes on the Connaught Cir-cuit that he, with several persons unknown, feloniously broke open the house of Thomas Tennison, Esq., and thereout stole several articles of plate, wine, etc., to this he pleaded Not Guilty. At this stage it is to be pointed out that if the value of the property so stolen exceeded five shillings the penalty was death, so that Mr. McDiarmad found himself in a highly embarrassing situation.

The case for the Crown was opened by junior counsel, and his learned leader, we are informed, followed with great ability and ingenuity. After a large body of evidence had been adduced on either side the Chief Baron addressed the jury with learning and discrimination and they were invited to retire to their deliberations at 10 p.m. After they were out for some time, in view of the lateness of the hour, a point was stretched and they were permitted to reassemble in the morning. Morning duly came, and forenoon, and afternoon, but still despite repeated judicial inquiries, no jury emerged from its fastness. At half past two his lordship caused a message to be sent that the carts would be available to transport them to the limits of the county at precisely three o'clock.

This information produced an effect. The weather was as foul as Connaught weather can be, which is a large statement, and the majority now became determined to enforce their views on the minority in as forceful a manner as would ensure a decision. The foreman in the strongest terms enjoined the intransigents to give way and agree to a verdict of Guilty. They spiritedly refused to do so. The upshot was dramatic. A free-for-all broke out and the only available weapons, the chairs and the fire-irons, were used so enthusiastically that none of the combatants was unscathed. This uproar was heard in the Court whereupon the attendants, with the aid of some soldiers, broke open the jury room and dragged the jurors into Court where they were barely restrained from continuing their battle. His lordship then addressed them in very definite terms, and they were led down, four at a time, to the three carts that awaited them.

These vehicles were equipped with solid wooden wheels revolving on fixed wooden axles, and the cavalcade bumped in the rain over the potholes, cobbles and mud of the town, attended by the mounted Sheriff and a troop of the 14th Light Dragoons. As the procession was leaving the town the pro-acquitters consented to finding the accused Guilty of stealing property to the amount of 4/9d, to which compromise their colleagues were by now glad to assent. Alas!

90

they were too late for the Chief Baron had by now departed the town, and they were left with another eight hours progress to the county Galway border in which to ponder the hard cases that make the law.

Although in these duller days the Carting of Juries has fallen into desuetude, a disagreement frequently occasions the outspoken choler of the Bench. This is not surprising as it entails considerable additional time and expense, the resummoning of witnesses, jurors, etc. and further suspense, often in custody, for the prisoner. It is inherent in the injustice of things that the judicial ire is sometimes misdirected, and probably every assize town could reproduce the following memoir of the late Mr. Justice Andrews.

This Judge, who was the terror of prisoners, came on Assizes to Lifford, then the assize town for the County of Donegal, a county it may be observed which was never remarkable for the number of convictions it produced. An extremely strong case of attempted murder and conspiracy was the first to be heard, and the Judge discharged an overhelming balaclava against the prisoners in the course of which he remarked that it was the clearest case he had ever tried. Notwithstanding, the jury, having retired for about an hour, returned to intimate that there was no possibility of an agreement. The Judge thereupon delivered himself of some vitriolic comments, which induced the foreman to inform him that the majority were very sorry but that one of their number was holding out obstinately against the other eleven. His lordship then wrathfully exclaimed: "All I have to say is that that juror is a disgrace to himself and his country, and is shamelessly violating the solemn oath he has taken."

At this a small bald-headed man sprang up and shrilly expostulated: "I'm the one man, and I'm the only one holding out for yer lordship, the rest are all for an acquittal."

Andrews, perhaps from the excess of his zeal, was singularly unfortunate in his juries, because if an Irishman dislikes an attempt to browbeat him, he will particularly resent anyone in authority trying to make his mind up for him, and will do the exact opposite. This applies to every part of the country, and Judge Andrews was to find that a Donegal jury in the extreme North, and a Kerry jury in the extreme South differed more in accent than in outlook.

For example, in Tralee in County Kerry he had occasion to try a prisoner for rape. Now, an ingenious counsel can make play with several defences to this charge, one of which is that a coy and token resistance to the blandishments of her swain does not necessarily mean that the lady is unwilling, which is an essential ingredient of the offence. Accordingly ardour in wooing, even vigorous ardour, does not amount to that degree of violence requisite to constitute this crime. This was the line that was persuasively adopted by counsel for the defence, but it failed to persuade the Right Honourable Mr. Justice Andrews who had heard it all before. In charging the jury he characterized the case as just about as bad a rape case as it had ever been his misfortune to try, aggravated as it was by the audacious line which was taken by the defence, which entailed an unwarranted reflection on the chastity of the prosecutrix. He thanked the jury for the close attention with which they had followed the proceedings, and felt that it would not take them long to arrive at a unanimous decision.

In this he was correct, because to his gratification they returned within a quarter of an hour. He was not so gratified, however, when the verdict of Not Guilty, on all counts, was announced to the Court.

When he recovered from his shock, he directed the discharge of the prisoner, and was about to stamp off the Bench when the foreman spoke to him, and this dialogue took place.

"Me Lard! Would your lardship consider excusing these men and meself from the jury for ten years."

"That is the most insolent and impertinent request I have ever heard in my long experience. And may I add that if it were in my power, it would give me pleasure to sentence you all to ten years for perverting the course of justice by bringing in such an outrageous verdict."

"I don't know why you say that, me Lard," replied the unperturbed spokesman, "shure, we are all unanimously agreed that there was no more force used on the girl than was reasonably necessary in the circumstances."

This application of the law to the facts effectively silenced his lordship. He later had a sort of vicarious revenge in the adjoining county. In discharging from the dock a prisoner who had just become the beneficiary of a verdict found in the teeth of the evidence and the Judge's charge, Andrews addressed him with unwonted unction:

"Prisoner at the bar, you have now been found Not Guilty by the verdict of twelve of your fellow countrymen of the atrocious offences upon which you have been tried. Upon that verdict I do not propose to comment other than to observe that it compels me to direct your release from custody. You are, therefore, at liberty to leave the dock and take your place in society with no other stain on your character than that you have been acquitted by a Limerick jury."

The truth of the matter is that the jury system, certainly as operated, was quite unsuited to the administration of justice in Ireland. This applied, and still applies, to the country parts, where everyone knows everyone else and the evidence adduced in Court is frequently the last consideration to affect the result of a trial.

Every period of Irish legal history affords innumerable examples of this perversity, so many that two or three may be cited, not as typical of them all, for they have an infinite variety, but as typical of the countryman's attitude to the evidence as distinct from the real *ratio decidendi*.

For instance, quite recently in the County of Donegal four young men were charged with the commission of a crime of which they were so apparently guilty that the trial seemed a mere formality. To everyone's astonishment, and not least the prisoners', they were all acquitted. When he had disrobed, the defending counsel was invited by his instructing solicitor for a congratulatory drink in a nearby hostelry. He modestly disclaimed the comparisons which his companion was making between himself and the great advocates of past and present. This pleasant euphoria was suddenly interrupted

93

by a strange countryman coming over to them with his hand outstretched, "Put it there, Counsellor, that was a great bloody speech you made over there beyond in the Courthouse."

"That's very kind of you, sir. Incidentally, haven't I seen you somewhere before?"

"I'm damn sure you have, wasn't I on the jury."

"That is very interesting. Tell me, was it my cross-examination or my speech that made you acquit?"

"Well, I wouldn't be inclined to say, sir. You see I live in the same townland as them four young fellas, and I can tell you that they are the greatest blackguards in the nation, and so is everyone belonging to them. It's all fine and well for the oul' Judge, but if anyone thinks that I'm looking to have my house going up in flames over the top of my head he'd better do another bit of thinking. It was a bloody fine speech, all the same, sir."

Different considerations affected the jury in a case on the Western Circuit around about the same time.

In similar circumstances a juryman approached the gratified defence counsel and was asked for a similar enlightenment. As so often in Ireland, the reply was in the form of a question:

"Tell me, sir, if we had found your man Guilty, what would the oul' Judge have given him?"

"Well, I don't know. It was a pretty serious case. I suppose anything from five to seven years."

"That's what we were thinking ourselves."

"So you decided to be merciful?"

"Merciful be damned! I saw by the papers that it costs over twenty quid a week to keep a man in prison. I can tell you, sir, that we had no call to throw away about five or six thousand quid of the ratepayers' money just to maintain a good-for-nothing, useless blackguard like that fella you were defending."

Reference has been made to the surprising fact that no qualification other than that of being a property owner, however small, is required of a juryman. This can lead to results which are either amusing or infuriating, depending on whether one is to the windward or the leeward of the law.

It should be noted that in Ireland the foreman of the jury is the first man whose name is called and who first enters the box. The law assumes that this gentleman is equipped to discharge the not very onerous duties which his lot entails on him, an assumption not always warranted in the event.

A few years ago in Wicklow a rate-collector was indicted and tried for a series of offences involving the wrongful conversion of monies which had come under his control in respect of rates due to the County Council. Generally speaking, there is an element of drama in most criminal trials. This type of case, however, is incomparably tedious. There are usually a multiplicity of charges involving the formal proof of hundreds of documents such as rate books, ledgers, receipts, bank books and so on, which are proved by accountants, audit clerks and the like in what seems an unending procession. This case was no exception and at the end of the fourth day, when the prosecution had closed its case, the Courtroom looked as though it had been subjected to a paper blitz by a number of heavy bombers. Of course, every single document immediately on being proved had been submitted to the careful scrutiny of the individual members of the jury, and its effect duly noted.

It was at this juncture that the defending counsel rose and submitted to the Court that the State had failed to make out its case on a great number of the various counts in the indictment, of which there were a few hundred. After considerable argument, to which the jury paid close attention, the defence contentions prevailed in regard to ninety-seven charges, thereby occasioning a fantasy between the Bench and the Foreman of which Lewis Carroll would not have been ashamed :

HIS LORDSHIP : Please stand up, Mr. Foreman. The County Registrar will now hand you the issue paper. Do you understand me?

FOREMAN: Yes, my lord.

HIS LORDSHIP: You see that he has put pencil marks on those documents you hold in your hand?

FOREMAN: Yes, my lord.

HIS LORDSHIP: Very well. Now, Mr. Foreman, will you please be so good as to write on the space opposite each pencil mark "Not Guilty by direction of the Court".

FOREMAN: I'm sorry, I can't do that.

HIS LORDSHIP: Hold your tongue and do not be insolent. I am directing you to do it, and you will sign your name opposite each entry also. Will you do that at once, sir.

FOREMAN: No, my Lord.

HIS LORDSHIP: Believe me, I have very wide powers, and I am warning you if you do not obey me at once I will exercise them in a way you will never forget.

FOREMAN: I'm sorry, my Lord, I don't want to be disrespectful, but my Lord, sir, I'm not much of a scholar. God help me, sir, I was never taught to read or write.

Even when the good men and true come in with a unanimous verdict its construction often defeats the most acute judicial minds. As good a poser of this nature as any was supplied by a Tyrone jury in a case where the prisoner had nearly killed a man with a blow of a hurley stick on the head, and the verdict was:

"We find the prisoner Guilty, but we recommend him to mercy on account of his good character, and because he was justified in all he did."

The judge expressed himself unable to accept this verdict but no inducement would make the jury change so in the upshot there was a disagreement.

One leaves the subject of Irish juries with reluctance, but a large volume could be written about them and still only scratch the surface. When it is considered that the average jury consists of twelve diverse individuals, fortuitously drawn together in an artificial association to decide between conflicting stories upon which different complexions are placed by trained advocates, and in accordance with a set of rules of which they are profoundly ignorant, it can be appreciated that the system supplies a field of legal lore which is inexhaustible.

The tricks and artistries of advocacy which are designed to persuade an Irish jury, legitimately or otherwise, are almost without number. In this regard it would be remiss to omit a passing reference to Daniel O'Connell, the greatest jury advocate of them all, even if only one example of his technique with an adverse jury must suffice.

O'Connell was defending a hot-tempered journalist, who had frequently attacked the Cork Corporation, on a charge of assault which arose from the fact that in a rush from a theatre he had broken a rib of the High Sheriff. Although there was no clear evidence of intent, O'Connell knew that the jury were antagonistic to his client. In a most casual way he asked a few questions designed to show that the whole thing might easily have been accidental, and when it came to his turn to close the case he said that as he did not feel inclined to make a speech he would tell them a story instead.

He then related a case which he said he had once witnessed at the Clonmel Assizes. The prisoner was accused of murdering his neighbour, and it appeared that an ancient feud had existed between them. The prisoner had more than once used violence against the man he was accused of murdering, had been heard vowing vengeance against him, and had been seen following him on the very road where he was found murdered. The victim's face was so beaten in by a stone that he could only be identified by his dress. The chain of circumstantial evidence seemed to be unbreakable and conviction inevitable when the accused called his witness—the very man he was alleged to have murdered. It was in this way established that some unknown man had been murdered that night. The presumed victim had received a hint that he was about to be arrested for a Whiteboy offence, and had fled in terror, but on hearing that his old antagonist was being tried for his life on account of him, he courageously returned.

The Judge said that in so clear a case it was unnecessary

for him to charge him, when to his amazement the jury asked leave to retire and, to his still greater surprise, returned a verdict of Guilty.

"Good God," exclaimed the Judge, "of what is he guilty —surely not of murder?"

"No, my lord," replied the foreman, "but he stole my grey mare three years ago."

The Cork jury were convulsed with laughter, and O'Connell changed his tone and said: "So gentlemen of the jury, if my client did not wilfully assault the Sheriff, he has insulted the Corporation. Find him guilty by all means."

The verdict, not surprisingly, was an acquittal.

Incidentally, the apocryphal story which O'Connell told was duplicated in real life with a grimmer result many years later in the same province.

In case there should be any misapprehension it is as well to set out the formula of the oath which in Ireland is taken by every juryman. It is in the following form:

"I swear by Almighty God that I will well and truly try the issues between the State and the accused which are given me to try, and a true verdict give according to the evidence."

# 7

# *So Great a Cloud!*

From the subject of Irish juries one naturally turns to the abundant sources which supply the evidence upon which their verdicts are in theory founded—the witnesses.

It is as unsafe to generalize about typical Irish witnesses as it is about any other subject, because they are as various, if not as beautiful, as the ever changing colours on their native mountains on a summer's day. With that reservation it is permissible to say at once that any similarity between the attitude of an Irish witness and his English counterpart in regard to the evidence he gives is superficial and misleading. It was neatly summed up by an Irish witness who, when giving some highly imaginative evidence in the Royal Courts of Justice, was asked by the then Mr. Justice Darling: "Tell me, what happens in your country when a witness does not tell the truth?" replied "Begod, his side generally wins." While that admirably epitomises the attitude it does not express the fact, for it leaves out of account the consideration that the opposing witnesses will probably not tell the truth either.

The reasons for this cavalier disregard for the solemnity of giving sworn evidence are probably partly to be found in the history of the Irish legal system, and partly in the Irish temperament itself. Whereas the average Englishman looks upon an appearance in the witness box as only one degree worse than actually standing in the dock, the average Irishman frequently regards it as an excellent opportunity to match his wits against his opponents, which term embraces everyone connected with the side adverse to that for which he is called. If the truth suffers in the process, so much the worse for the truth. Nor is there often any real consciousness of doing wrong, and most practitioners at the Bar will agree that throughout the country the oath is regarded more as a kind of legalistic formality than an obligation. This was certainly the view of the late Mr. Justice Dixon who, when he was Attorney General, publicly advocated the abolition of the oath altogether on the very reasonable grounds that its universal disregard was bringing the law itself into contempt.

A sublime example of the heights or depths which this contempt can achieve is afforded by a case in which one of the most experienced and amusing solicitors in the North West was engaged a few years ago.

One morning a cattle dealer who was not a regular client, but for whom he had recently acted, came into his office and told him he would like him to look after all his legal affairs in future. When he asked the wherefore of this flattering retainer he was informed, "Because that was a hell of a case you fought for me the other day beyond in Kinlough."

This referred to a case in which the dealer was sued in the District Court for forty-five pounds, being the price of a bullock which he was alleged to have bought from another dealer at the Kinlough fair, and for which he had not paid. The successful defence was that an hour or so after the sale the money had been paid in notes in a public house, to which payment there were several witnesses, who gave evidence.

"Oh, I don't know," said the solicitor, "it was a fairly simple case. After all you had a strong team of witnesses to prove the payment."

"Well I'll tell you, sir, it wasn't just as simple a case as you think. Would you like to hear the truth about it?"

"I was under the obviously mistaken impression that we heard the truth about it in the Court."

"Begod, you were mistaken all right, because there wasn't one word of truth spoken in the Court that day. I'll tell you the truth now. A couple of years ago myself and the Plaintiff had a bit of an argument over the price of a beast, and between the hopping and the trotting there were a few blows struck. In the heel of the hunt, your man says to me 'I'll get you yet for this, you bastard'. So when I got the law paper looking for forty-five quid, says I to myself he's out to get me sure enough. Now I'll tell you the God's truth, sir, I was never at the fair in Kinlough at all the day he said I bought the beast, and he wasn't at the fair neither."

"Just a second," interrupted the astonished solicitor, "am I to understand that there was no beast, no bargain, no sale, no payment, in fact, no transaction at all?"

"You have it right, sir."

"Then why in the name of goodness, did you not instruct me to make that case for you?"

"Do you think I'm stone mad? Didn't I know damn well that he'd call a flock of blackguards to say I bought a beast from him at the Kinlough fair and didn't pay for it. And didn't I know damn well that if I was the only one to say that there was no beast in it at all, at all, and it never happened, no one would believe me. So said I to myself, the only reasonable thing to do is get a few decent men to say that they saw me paying him forty-five quid for the animal beyond in the pub. And you know the rest of the story yourself, sir, because you fought a real good case for me, and I'd like you to be acting for me from now on."

It may be commented that in all probability the defendant had adopted the only course by which his case could have been won.

Now it is not to be suggested that the general run of witnesses will go quite as far as this—except, of course, in dire extremity. What is far more normal, almost common form, is evasion, equivocation and ambiguity, and above all the technique of starry-eyed innocence generally based on an affectation of illiteracy or ignorance. The result is a series of elaborate answers to questions that have not been asked, and generally the creation of a cloud-cuckoo-land of irrelevancy which would daze an English counsel and drive an English judge to the verge of insanity. All, of course, has the designed purpose of so obscuring the issues that at best the case never gets back on the rails at all, or at worst the witness gets a respite of about ten minutes to think out a plausible explanation.

This sort of thing naturally calls for an artistry in the advocate which he would not acquire in the groves of Academe or the cloistered atmosphere of the Inns of Court. As, for example, a case which came on appeal at the Sligo Assizes.

In this great cause, a farm labourer claimed one hundred and thirty-four pounds back wages which he alleged were due to him by his employers, an old farmer and his wife, and which he said they wrongfully withheld. Despite the fact that a receipt for the amount, bearing his signature, had been produced in the Court below, the Circuit Court Judge accepted his story, and from his decision the defendants appealed. The appeal came before Mr. Justice John O'Byrne, perhaps the most astute judge on the Bench, and in cross-examination of the Plaintiff the following passage took place:

COUNSEL: Take this receipt in your hand and look at it.

WITNESS: I'm not a scholar like you, sir.

COUNSEL: Whether you are a scholar like me or not, tell the Court whether or not that is your signature?

WITNESS: It couldn't be, sir.

COUNSEL: Why couldn't it be?

WITNESS: Because I never wrote my name in my life, because I can't.

COUNSEL: Then you say it is a forgery?

WITNESS: What class of a thing would that be, sir?

COUNSEL: Are you suggesting that this old man or his wife

deliberately put your name on this paper to do you out of your money?

WITNESS: They might, then.

COUNSEL: You say you can't write. Can you read at all?

WITNESS: I cannot then, I tell you, sir, I'm no scholar.

COUNSEL: And you never even look at the newspapers?

WITNESS: What would the likes of me be looking at papers for?

COUNSEL: Well be good enough to look at this paper.

It is regrettable to have to record that learned counsel, like so many of his colleagues, had interests not altogether consistent with a strict application to the practice of his profession. It happened to be the day of a big race at the Curragh, and beside him on his seat was the daily paper opened at the racing page which prominently featured a large action photograph of the favourite. Picking it up he handed it to the witness upside down.

COUNSEL: Now, tell us if that paper means anything to you.

WITNESS: Sure, I don't understand it at all, sir.

COUNSEL: You don't see anything on it that means anything to you?

WITNESS: (Still looking at it upside down) Not a thing, sir.

It is hardly necessary to say that if even a child will look at a picture book right side up, how much more so a farm worker who has been brought up with horses and would discuss their points gladly for hours on end.

COUNSEL: Will you please be so good as to hand that paper up to his lordship exactly as you are holding it . . .

(The witness did so, the paper still upside down.)

COUNSEL: . . . may it please your lordship—

JUDGE: You need not elaborate. Leave the box, you black-guard, and consider yourself lucky that I do not send you to Sligo gaol. I allow this appeal without hesitation. Is it worth while my making an order for costs?

COUNSEL: Well he may not have spent all the hundred and thirty-four pounds.

JUDGE: Very well, allow the appeal, dismiss the Plaintiff's

claim with costs in this Court and the Court below. Next case, please.

Not all cross-examinations of alleged illiterates are illuminated by such timely brain-waves. Generally, they end in the frustration equally of the Court and the ends of Justice, and there is no doubt that the dice are heavily loaded in favour of such witnesses. It is fatal to browbeat them because the jury will be antagonized and to be sweetly reasonable creates a fog of repetitious questions, answers and explanations that would reduce a Demosthenes to incoherence.

Nowadays, with compulsory school attendance, this sort of thing is becoming rarer, but the evasive witness will always be with us. The most notable characteristic of this permanent adornment of the courts lies in his congenital incapacity to pronounce the monosyllables "yes" or "no", and weird and wonderful are his verbal acrobatics in avoiding such fatal precision. The classic example of equivocation which has often been told, but bears repetition, occurred in a will case in which Daniel O'Connell was engaged.

There used to be in those days, as indeed there may still be, a pleasant practice which was resorted to by forgers of testamentory documents. This consisted of placing a pen in the hand of the corpse and so signing his name to the will, thereby enabling the witness to swear that it had been signed by the hand of the testator.

O'Connell had been retained in a case in which his clients alleged that the document was a forgery. The witnesses to the will swore that it had been signed by the hand of the testator while "life was in him". This phrase is the literal translation from the Irish into the English language, and is still in common usage even in districts where Irish has not been spoken for generations. The evidence had gone entirely in favour of the validity of the will when O'Connell stood up to cross-examine the star witness for the defendants:

O'CONNELL: On your oath was the man alive?

WITNESS: By virtue of my oath, the life was in him.

O'CONNELL: Now, sir, I solemnly ask you—and answer me

104

at your peril—did you not place a live fly in the dead man's mouth when his hand was placed on this will?

The terror-stricken witness stumbled and stammered and finally admitted that he had indeed adopted this far-seeing expedient.

The bogus defence par excellence in Ireland is the alibi. It has the great advantage that if it is successfully put forward it is the perfect defence. As Sir Boyle Roche observed, "How can I be in two places at the same time, unless I am a bird?" On the other hand, if an alibi fails to stand up it has the corresponding and fatal disadvantage of depriving the accused of any other recourse. It does not require any great legal acumen to see that a jury is unlikely to be impressed by the explanation "I did not do it because I say I was not there, but alternatively even if I was there, I did not do it."

The classical mode of breaking down a false alibi is for the cross-examining counsel to have the other witnesses excluded from the Court while each of his fellows is in the box. The cross-examination is then directed not to the facts surrounding the main issues. These anticipated questions and answers will have been rehearsed and agreed on for weeks before the trial, and the effect of such a line will be merely to strengthen the defence story. The skilled operator will concentrate on trivialities collateral to the issue of which the truthful witness should be aware, but which will not have been foreseen as arising in the case. In this way it is not difficult to involve a series of witnesses who have not heard each other's stories, in a miasma of mutual contradictions.

Irish witnesses, from long and unfortunate experience, became well aware of the devastating effect of such unfair forensic methods. To counteract them much anxious research and field-work was resorted to until finally was born the Kerry Alibi which, like all discoveries of genius, is beautiful in its simplicity. Where this defence is adopted counsel may cross-examine until he is blue in the face without eliciting any contradiction in the least damaging to the exculpatory story. All the small occurrences and incidents to which he directs his artillery, such as whom the witness met, what was talked about, where he went, what he had to drink, what the accused was wearing and so on, will all be met with the frankest and most circumstantial answers. The consistency of the evidence of the various witnesses will create a tapestry of shining and incontrovertible truth. And the witnesses will have been telling the truth about everything—that is with the exception of one small particular. Their story will relate not to the circumstances surrounding the date or time of the crime in respect of which the alibi is put forward, but to a different day altogether when nothing sinister was done by anybody.

While Kerry can proudly claim to be the county in which this counterblast to objectionable inquisitions was conceived, its advantages were so manifest that the rest of the country quickly adopted it. One of the best known instances of the operation of the Kerry Alibi took place in the adjoining county of Cork.

The accused on that occasion was charged with an attempted murder which took place on October 4. Although evidence of identification was not too incriminating, the attacker being in disguise, the other circumstantial evidence was very strong in placing the prisoner at the scene of the crime, and the Judge had made clear what his personal views were. Defence counsel, however, announced that he would call only one witness who, he was satisfied, would put the case beyond all reasonable doubt in favour of the prisoner. This proved to be an Englishman called Townsend, the Earl of Bandon's agent, and a gentleman who would be the last in the County Cork to condone an agrarian crime. His direct evidence was short, but compelling:

COUNSEL: Mr. Townsend, do you remember Tuesday the 4th of October last?

TOWNSEND: I do, very well.

COUNSEL: Would you please describe your movements on that day.

TOWNSEND: Yes. I was driven out to the neighbourhood of

106

Macroom and was in that part of the country from nine in the morning until about half-past six.

COUNSEL: Who was your driver?

TOWNSEND: The prisoner.

COUNSEL: Could he have been anywhere near Riverstown that day at two o'clock?

TOWNSEND: Absolutely impossible.

This apparently coercive evidence, emanating as it did from an impeccable source, naturally impelled the Judge to charge the jury to acquit. This they did without leaving their box and his lordship, in directing the discharge of the accused, took the opportunity of profusely thanking the public-spirited Mr. Townsend who had so providentially prevented a miscarriage of justice.

The prisoner's counsel was nonplussed. On the one hand, there was Townsend's evidence which could not possibly be tainted, on the other, his own private conviction of his client's guilt. That night when pondering over the apparently irreconcilable, he remembered that his instructing solicitor had been most insistent that his first question must be couched in the form, "Do you remember Tuesday the 4th of October last? He pulled out his diary and opened it for the month of October.

The 4th was a Wednesday.

An extension of this admirable type of defence is the Tipperary Alibi. This takes the form of proving through a succession of eye witnesses that the prosecution witness who is the lynch-pin of the State's case was not present at all at the place he had sworn he was, at the date of the crime. While this has all the happy consequences of its Kerry counterpart, it also has two additional advantages. It invariably takes the prosecution by surprise at the trial, as it cannot be anticipated even on the closest reading of the depositions if no questions have been asked at the preliminary hearing; but above all, it makes out the star witness against the prisoner to be an unmitigated and unprincipled liar, with the side effect of colouring every word of evidence adduced by the prosecution.

The inferiority, to the Kerry or Tipperary ingenuities, of the ordinary kind of alibi, however elaborate, vulnerable as it is to the conventional forms of attack by prosecuting counsel, has never been more strikingly illustrated than in the trial of Thomas Kelly for the murder of Patrick Henry.

This was one of the most extraordinary cases in the modern criminal calendar, and indeed so fascinated Francis Hackett, the historian and novelist, that he attended each day of the three trials and was beginning a book about them when he died.

The victim of this sordid, and at first sight unremarkable, crime was an old man in his eighties called Patrick Henry who lived in a small detached county council cottage on the outskirts of Boyle in County Roscommon. Henry was a miser and a recluse, his only companion being a powerfully built, middle-aged Irish-American called Thomas Kelly who lived with him from the month of May 1935 until September 10 1935. On that date between 7–8 p.m. Henry was seen entering his house, and it was the prosecution's case that he was never seen alive again.

The following day, the 11th, the accused was seen leaving the house between 1–2 p.m. and on that afternoon he took the bus to Sligo, about 25 miles away, where he stayed the night. The following day, as later inquiries ascertained, he placed £80 on deposit in the Hibernian Bank in Sligo—a circumstance on which the defence were to make great play. He then went to Belfast where he stayed in a lodging house for a week, and thence he went to Scotland where all trace of him was lost. His description was circulated all over Great Britain and Ireland and a large reward offered but he had disappeared completely.

On June 2 1936, a man entered the Cowdenbeath branch of the Commercial Bank of Scotland and presented a deposit receipt for £80 issued by the Hibernian Bank, Sligo. The manager informed the presentor that this would have to be collected, and to return in three days' time. On June 5 he, Thomas Kelly, did return, to be met by two Irish detectives who arrested him, whereupon he tried to cut his throat with a safety razor-blade.

In the meantime, on the previous December 13, the Irish police (Civic Guard) had broken into Patrick Henry's house where they found his body badly battered around the head. The blows appeared to have been delivered when the old man had been sitting at the fire. The upper part of the body and head, which was lying in the fireplace, was partially burned away. The furniture was undisturbed, indicating that there was no struggle and that someone well known to the dead man had committed the crime. There was no evidence of the cottage being ransacked, although a thorough search disclosed absolutely no money despite the fact that the deceased was known to have had at least £600 in his possession.

Although this deadly evidence was presented at the first trial, which took place at Green Street before Mr. Justice O'Byrne, four witnesses came forward to swear that old Henry had been seen by them at the Boyle Agricultural Show which took place on September 12. If accepted, this evidence would completely exonerate Kelly. The jury, however, rejected it, and Kelly was sentenced to death.

An appeal was then taken on the grounds that since conviction seven further witnesses had sworn affidavits that they also had seen Patrick Henry alive on September 12, and in the light of this additional evidence they asked for a fresh trial. This was vigorously opposed by the prosecution but the Court of Criminal Appeal, in view of the fact that a man's life was at stake, adjourned the appeal to hear these witnesses, and decide whether their evidence was such as might affect a jury's verdict. This course was unprecedented, and has never since been adopted in any other case.

On January 25 and 26 1937 the Appeal Court heard the seven new witnesses, one of whom actually swore that he had not only seen, but had been speaking to, the deceased on September 12 1935. The Court, without expressing any view

109

as to its belief in the fresh evidence, directed a new trial. This trial was held in April before Mr. Justice Hanna, and having heard the eleven alibi witnesses, the jury disagreed and Kelly had to undergo his ordeal yet again.

The third trial came off in the Michaelmas Term 1937 before Mr. Justice Gavan Duffy. By this time the State had had the best part of a year to check on the stories of the witnesses. Martin Maguire and his junior, Kevin Haugh, both to become Supreme Court Judges, subjected each of the eleven witnesses to rigorous cross-examination. Their evidence was utterly discredited and again Kelly was sentenced to death.

The sentence was never executed. Despite the failure of his appeal, and the treacherous brutality of his murder of a defenceless old man, Kelly was reprieved. The reason for this mercy must presumably be ascribed to the length of the proceedings and the mental anguish caused to him, culminating in the final death sentence. In his persistence he was certainly more fortunate than Caryl Chessman. Indeed, it is ironical to reflect that when he was ultimately released, Kelly had outlived the three judges who had tried him, all the judges who sat on his appeals, the Chief State Solicitor in charge of his prosecution, his own solicitor and both his defending counsel.

The defence witnesses would earn and deserve the pained strictures of the experts brought up in the Kerry school. While it was quite legitimate, if unnecessary, to place the deceased Henry as being present at the Show, it would have been better to have picked on some less notable day; they should have transferred that imaginary appearance to an earlier and actual one, to which they could all factually depose. Possibly it was felt that sheer weight of numbers would overwhelm probability; an inartistic attitude which would not recommend itself to either the Kerry or Tipperary purist.

At this stage, perhaps it is not inopportune to observe that before the righteous become too severe on the aberrations of Irish witnesses they should consider the traditional contempt and hatred of the people for a legal system, from the benefits of which they were debarred and to the rigours of which they were subjected. It should, in fairness, never be forgotten that a great deal of the evasion, ambiguity and even perjury of witnesses stems from no more culpable a source than the ingrained instinct of self-preservation against a ruling establishment which itself invoked the forms of law to effect the prostitution of justice.

In the eyes of the Irish the absolute nadir of baseness and perfidy of this kind to which the Crown could descend was the employment of informers to obtain convictions. These wretches were usually paid for their services, but frequently they gave evidence in return for guarantees of immunity from punishment for their own atrocities, which as often as not, were the very crimes in which they had engaged with the prisoners in the dock. This sort of thing was in all conscience revolting enough, but when criminal informers swore to the commission of crimes of which the accused were entirely innocent, or which perhaps had never been committed at all, as in Sheehy's case, then it could well be said that affrighted Justice shrieked. It is hardly to be wondered at that these and similar perversions of legal process should give rise to situations in which attack was met by defence in kind, in which conflict truth in the Irish witness box became the most notable and permanent casualty.

The catalogue of Irish informers can never be definitively compiled, for obvious reasons. An idea of their numbers, and of their importance to the criminal administration, can, however, be inferred from the length of the melancholy procession which, to obtain convictions, the Crown was forced to parade to public obloquy through the witness-box. Of this ignoble company, while it should perhaps be said that all had in common a denominator of treachery, some, in addition, embellished their wickedness with such a cold-blooded malevolence as to achieve an infamy of almost satanic perfection.

There are unfortunately a great number of informers who earn the right of dishonourable mention in this last category, but even the shortest list would include the euphonious name of Captain John Warenford Armstrong who brought the Sheares brothers to the scaffold. Armstrong was an officer in the King's County Militia, a body which had inspired General Abercrombie to observe that they were formidable to everyone save the enemy. In the aftermath of the recent insurrection, when all danger had passed, he had distinguished himself in the number of atrocities he ordered, and himself committed, on the civilian population—a distinction which at the time was not easily won. From sadism and murder he turned his hand to treachery with a similar success.

There can be no doubt of the guilt of the brothers Henry and John Sheares, who after the arrest of its leading members took over the direction of the executive directory of the United Irishmen, a precarious authority which they exercised for only ten days before they, in turn, were taken. What nauseated the people, and marked their trial with an indelible stain, was not the fact of their conviction, but the methods through which it was obtained.

Both brothers were indiscreet, and in the shop of a radical Dublin bookseller were wont to air republican opinions which did not pass unnoticed in Dublin Castle. At, it is said, the instigation of Castlereagh, certainly with his connivance, Armstrong, professing himself a kindred spirit, became the repository of their incriminatory confidences. He so ingratiated himself as soon to be enjoying the intimacy of their home, where he encouraged their political projects and even supplied military information to enable the drawing up of a plan to capture the camp of his own regiment. In return, the artless pair disclosed the inner secrets of their Society which were immediately placed before the Castle.

On their last night of liberty the Sheares gave a little family dinner party, the only other guest being their new-found friend. Before the party went down to dinner Armstrong played with Henry's children, dandling the smaller ones on his knee, and telling them fairy tales. At dinner he toasted Henry's wife and old mother, protesting his tender affection for the whole family. He was a man of some education, and

112

one wonders if he recalled another and better known supper in Jerusalem.

The following morning the brothers Henry and John Sheares were arrested by the Town Major who seized their effects—among which were documents treasonable enough to hang them twenty times over. Their friend Armstrong was admitted to Newgate to condole with them, to carry messages from the prison to the womenfolk and children, and to assassinate them with his oath. In the witness box the Captain, as befitted his military discipline, was cool and, despite a shattering cross-examination, for the most part imperturbable. He admitted everything except fondling the little children; such an imputation against his character, he protested, was unwarranted and unjust.

The brothers Sheares were hanged and beheaded and, their blood being attainted with treason, the children were left destitute. For the Captain, however, the event was happier than for his predecessor; for him there was no Potter's Field. The reward was also considerably higher. Fifty years later, long since a man of property and a Justice of the Peace, he could be seen, a well set-up military figure, emerging from Dublin Castle having drawn the annual bounty bestowed on him by a grateful Government.

Armstrong was an adventurer. His successor in the witness-box, Thomas Reynolds of Kildare, was a gentleman, withal a little shop-soiled. He was the brother-in-law of Wolfe Tone, and at the time of his apogee twenty-seven years of age. His years, however, belied his parts and his achievements, for he was not unversed in the way of the world. His experiences included poisoning his mother-in-law, robbing his mother, ruining his own family and swindling a blind woman of her savings. Having joined the United Irishmen he next embarked on the career of informer for which role he immediately displayed a natural talent, although in Court his former activities were the subject of some embarrassing comment. In fact, he was referred to as "base, attainted, unfounded, and perjured, the foresaken prostitute of every vice".

Reynolds was not forsaken. When his services had hanged his victims, he was spirited out of the country for his own safety, the pangs of his exile being partly assuaged with a lump sum of £6,000, a Government office and a pension. His last appearance in the lists of the law was in 1817 as a member of the Grand Jury of Middlesex which returned true bills against Watson and others for high treason.

Not all informers were so fortunate in their rewards as Armstrong and Reynolds. In putting forward James O'Brien the Government overplayed their hand, and when even a packed jury revolted and acquitted, thereby saving seventeen lives from the gallows, O'Brien's employers having no further use for him, allowed him to be prosecuted and hanged for murdering a cripple.

The list is almost interminable. Every period produced its Wheatleys and its Redmonds, its Masseys and its Corydons, its Careys and its Piggotts—a lamentable litany of odium, contempt and rage.

Not all the informers gave evidence in trials of a political nature. Throughout the last century, and indeed into the present, the criminal calendar was largely a reflection of what was, in effect, a state of warfare between the peasantry on the one side, and the landlords and their agents on the other. Often, the only evidence which could bring home an agrarian crime to the accused was that of an informer who was generally himself a participant, and who took his oath under a promise of pardon. This sort of evidence became such a common form of legal proof, that it produced a reaction against the administration of the entire penal code. The result was an extension of that conspiracy of silence which had at all times blanketed agrarian offences to cover crimes of any and every nature, and which were without any social significance whatsoever. This attitude naturally provided yet another fertile forcing ground in which the informer flourished. The most dreadful result was that, in addition to the conviction of the guilty, the innocent against whom the informer was forsworn time and again paid the price of his immunity. Examples of such injustices are legion, but perhaps the best documented and authenticated was the aftermath of the mass butchery in County Galway in August 1882 which has ever since been recorded in criminal history as The Maamtrasna Massacre.

Maamtrasna, where this dreadful crime was committed, lies deep in the Joyce country in the heart of Connemara. It stands at the head of a lonely glen running up from one of the remote inlets of Lough Mask and is approached by a mountain pass through a wild and savage country that was a fitting setting for the most appalling domestic crime in modern times in Ireland.

At the head of this lonely gorge there was a small farmhouse in which at the time of the murders lived the farmer John Joyce, aged fifty years, with his wife Brigid, forty-five, his mother, Margaret, who was over eighty, and three children, Michael, seventeen, Margaret, fourteen and Pat, nine. About midnight on August 17 1882 the entire family was butchered, with the exception of the two boys. These were left for dead but Michael lingered on until the following day when he died, and Pat, the nine-year-old, although badly wounded, managed to survive and eventually give evidence. The weapons employed were heavy stones, cudgels and knives, and the imagination revolts from the thought of the shambles in which Pat found himself when he recovered consciousness. Perhaps it was most vividly described by one of the police constables who said that it reminded him of a cattle slaughter-house at the end of a heavy day.

The arrests were made three days later and the case, for outsiders, immediately became complicated by the identicality of so many of the names of the parties and witnesses to the crime. This difficulty is very common in remote parts of the country where intermarriage has taken place for so many generations that not only surnames, but Christian names also, are the same. The country people themselves are forced to resort to nicknames, or to adding the Christian names of the ancestors. For example, a John Joyce might be identified by being known as Johnny Michael Peg, which would mean he was the son of Michael who, in turn, was the son of Peg.

Altogether ten arrests were made on informations sworn by two brothers, John and Anthony Joyce, and warrants were issued for three others who escaped and were never found. Under the Prevention of Crimes Act the prisoners were conveyed to Dublin to await their trial there. When in custody two of them, Anthony Philbin and Thomas Casey, concluded a bargain with the Crown whereby, having confessed their guilt, they were released and rewarded on condition of giving evidence at the trials of the other eight. These trials began on November 13 1882 in Green Street Courthouse, and Patrick Joyce, a young farmer, was the first to be arraigned. The most deadly evidence, apart from that of the approvers Philbin and Casey, was adduced against him. The jury took eight minutes to find him guilty.

Patrick Joyce was followed into the dock by Patrick Casey, and his suspense lasted a little longer, for the jury convicted after twelve minutes.

Finally Myles Joyce stood at the bar and counsel for the defence utterly demolished the prosecution evidence against him, to such an extent that the case should have been withdrawn from the jury. However, it was left to them, and in six minutes they found him guilty. Before being sentenced to death he made a most passionate declaration of his innocence, but to no avail.

The Crown now made overtures to the other five prisoners to induce them to plead guilty and go to gaol to avoid being hanged. Each of them saw his priest, and although four of them were innocent he strongly advised them to plead, otherwise on the informers' evidence they would certainly be found guilty and executed. This advice was followed and the Crown withdrew the murder charges, but accepted pleas of guilty of conspiracy. The upshot for those arrested for the Maamstrasna Murders was:

| | | |
|---|---|---|
| Patrick Joyce | hanged | *guilty* |
| Patrick Casey | hanged | *guilty* |
| Myles Joyce | hanged | *innocent* |
| Martin Joyce | penal servitude | *innocent* |
| Patrick Joyce | penal servitude | *innocent* |
| Thomas Joyce (his son) | penal servitude | *innocent* |
| John Casey (Little) | penal servitude | *innocent* |
| Michael Casey | penal servitude | *guilty* |

In addition, there were the three who were never brought to book:

| | | |
|---|---|---|
| John Casey (Big) leader of gang | escaped | *guilty* |
| John Casey (Junior) (his son) | escaped | *guilty* |
| Patrick Leyden | escaped | *guilty* |

And, finally the pardoned approvers, Anthony Philbin and Thomas Casey, both of whom were guilty.

It may be wondered how guilt or innocence can be so confidently ascribed to the foregoing. There is to be found in the archives of the National Library in Dublin, under reference number I.R.3431 H.I., a large volume in which is collected all the evidence given on deposition and on the trials. It is fully documented, giving all the affidavits and declarations of the accused, the approvers, the transactions in the House of Commons and with the Irish and English government authorities. Anyone with the curiosity and diligence to study the more than four hundred pages of small type will be satisfied that the terrible massacre at Maamtrasna bred a shocking series of injustices. Reduced to simple terms it is established now that of the eight guilty men, three escaped, two were rewarded, two hanged, and one gaoled; and of the five innocents, one was hanged, and four gaoled.

On December 15 1882 the two Joyces and Casey were hanged in Galway Jail. Patrick Joyce and Patrick Casey met their deaths firmly. Young Myles, who was only nineteen, protested his innocence right up to the last moment and died horribly. Marwood, whose fame rests so justly upon his original research into the scientific principles involved in gauging the correct length of the drop, was the hangman. On this occasion his execution fell short of its usual professional standard and when he pulled the lever young Myles's arm caught in the rope so that Marwood was forced to sit on the beam whence, as an eye-witness expressed it, he kicked his victim into eternity "with a curse".

The previous night the Sacraments of Penance and the Eucharist had been administered to the three condemned, and shortly afterwards Patrick Joyce and Casey made, and signed, what were called their dying declarations. In them they admitted their own guilt, but each exonerated Myles Joyce from any hand, act or part in the murders. The solemn circumstances of the making of these declarations were compelling in their truthfulness, and so the authorities must have felt because they immediately suppressed them. The fact of their being made, and their contents became known to Timothy Harrington, M.P., and in September 1883 he twice raised the matter in the Commons. On the first occasion he was evaded by Trevelyan, the Chief Secretary, and on the second the only satisfaction he obtained from the Prime Minister, Gladstone, was an unsolicited compliment to the Lord Lieutenant in which the G.O.M., referred to "the discretion and clemency with which he knew his noble friend, Earl Spencer, discharged his duties." That admirable discretion was exercised by denying the declarations to the public. But the case was neither dead nor buried. The most dramatic development was yet to come.

On August 8 1884 Doctor McEvilly, Bishop of Galway, was in the course of a tour of his diocese, in the chief centres of which he was administering the Sacrament of Confirmation. He was about to preach the sermon which usually concludes the solemnities when Thomas Casey marched up the aisle to the altar rails. Casey, whose conscience had at last begun to torture him, had been refused absolution for his sins until he made such reparation as he could for the crimes he had committed against the innocent. In the presence of

118

the Bishop and priests of the diocese, and before the whole congregation, he publicly confessed to his part in the massacre of the Joyce family and to his perjury at the ensuing trials. He specifically swore to the innocence of Myles, Martin, Patrick and Thomas Joyce (father and son) and John Casey (Little), and avowed that none of them had the least knowledge of, or part in, the murders. Finally, he implicated Anthony Philbin as being one of the murderers and of being equally a perjurer in the trials. Philbin later confessed to the truth of Thomas Casey's statements.

These sensational disclosures were brought before the House of Commons by the indefatigable Harrington, and he obtained from the Marquis of Hartington a promise on behalf of the Government that an inquiry would be conducted into them. Nothing, however, was done at this level.

For his own part, the Bishop brought the matter directly before the Lord Lieutenant. There ensued that typically frustrating correspondence which a bureaucracy knows how to conduct so well, when it is determined to wear out an unfortunate individual who is demanding justice. Finally, a more than usually forceful letter from His Lordship evoked a more than usually evasive reply from R. G. C. Hamilton, Earl Spencer's secretary, in which one thing at least was made clear: the case would not be re-opened. The letter finished by saying that the authorities were "satisfied that the statements of Casey and Philbin now made are wholly unreliable, and His Excellency feels that no grounds exist for interfering with the punishment imposed by the Courts, or the sentences now being served." He remained His Lordship's most humble and obedient servant, and five innocent men remained in gaol.

It would be extravagant to comment upon this dreadful case, other than to say that it brings out in the starkest relief practically every feature that disgraced the criminal code in both its punitive and protective aspects. It is as well to remember also that the murders were not inspired by any ebullition of social or political fury. The infection had spread deeper than that.

The alibi and informer witnesses were, in their different ways, the outstanding manifestations of the system which gave birth to them, and as such their importance must be emphasized. To suggest, however, that as a result of their activities all Irish witnesses disregard their oaths would be unfair. But it is fair to say that practically no witness gives his evidence impartially even, perhaps especially, the expert. The golden thread that runs through the evidence given in the Irish Courts is the dedication of the witness to the interests of the party for whom he is called. He is a member of a team and his object and duty, as he conceives it, is not to let down his side. One cross-examines at one's peril; unless the ground is clear and firm there are probably quicksands.

If it is dangerous to cross-examine an ordinary witness, it is doubly so to cross swords with one of the parties, unless his evidence in chief is so damaging as to leave everything to be gained and nothing to be lost. Very frequently, he will have deliberately underplayed his hand in his direct evidence in the hope that an unwary counsel will open up a topic which has not been stressed in the belief that the witness is afraid of it. One sublime example of this sort of thing enshrines a moral which should be inculcated into every student.

In an action for damages for personal injuries and the loss of a cow, the Defendant's counsel began his cross-examination of the Plaintiff:

COUNSEL: You have now informed us in reply to your counsel that you were seriously injured in the accident.

PLAINTIFF: I was so, and so was my heifer.

COUNSEL: Never mind your heifer. How do you reconcile your story now with your statement to my client immediately after the accident that there was nothing the matter with you?

PLAINTIFF: Well that's not the whole of the story.

COUNSEL: Did you say that or not?

PLAINTIFF: Well I did, but I want to explain—

(THE JUDGE to COUNSEL): You have reopened the question. The witness is entitled to explain his answer.

PLAINTIFF: Thank you sir. Well the truth of it is that I was driving the heifer along the road, minding our own business when that man over there came whipping around the corner at ninety miles an hour, and the next thing me and the heifer is lying in the ditch, and the pair of us pumping blood. With that your man got out of the car, and sez he to me, "That beast is badly injured", so he took a gun and shot her there and then in the ditch. Then he turns round and sez he, "Tell me, my man, would there be anything wrong with you?" and I sez to him "Begod, sir, I never felt better in my life!"

One final topic, as affecting witnesses, should be touched on. Lecky, it will be remembered, ended his famous stricture on legal administration by referring to the power which "appeal to religious passion has often had upon witnesses and juries." This was a well-founded observation at the time it was written and was valid for many years to come. It is no longer valid throughout the greater part of the country, the exception being that portion somewhat anomalously described as Northern Ireland. There, despite the best efforts of the judges, religious prejudice is a very live issue indeed with unfortunate repercussions. At the same time, it should be emphasized that the judiciary is in no way to blame, but not even the most impartial judge can expunge from the mind of a witness a prejudice which is rooted in sixteenth century intolerance.

Sometimes, however, this attitude has its amusing side, and Sir John Ross, the last Lord Chancellor, gives an excellent illustration. On one occasion he was trying a case of riot which had broken out on Christmas night among the servants of a large country house in the County Tyrone. The fracas had its genesis in a religious discussion in which theological views were rather forcibly expressed. The Catholic defence was largely grounded on the gross provocation which they alleged had been given by the Protestant housekeeper. The lady, in her cross-examination and with righteous indignation, gave her account of the affair:

"When the Romans had drunk a lot of whiskey punch, they started wondering how King William was getting on in Hell, where he'd been for more than two hundred years. And, indeed, I said very little. I only said, 'King Billy is not in Hell, there's no room for him there, it's that full of Popes.' "

# 8

# *Shallows of Justice*

The most effective instruments for the
execution of a policy, which for centuries was nicely designed
to deprive the mass of the people from the assertion of their
legal rights, were to be found in the ranks of the Irish Magistracy. Very often this result was achieved not in the cause
of deliberate injustice, but because of the invincible ignorance of the very rudiments of the law which a pleasant fiction
maintained was administered by the Justices of the Peace.

The antecessors of the Justices of the Peace were known
as Conservators of the Peace and were creations of the Common Law. They were of two kinds, those who incidentally
to their offices were charged to preserve the peace, and now
include such as judges, and coroners; the second class were
constituted for that purpose only, and in 1326 were designated Keepers of the Peace, acquiring the title of Justices in
the reign of Edward III. In Ireland they were unknown until
the reign of Henry VI, from which time they were appointed
either by Statute, Charter or under the Great Seal. Charter
Justices were abolished in 1833, but three years later the Lord
Lieutenant, which in fact meant the Chief Secretary, was
empowered to appoint magistrates by warrant under his hand
and seal, and dismiss them at his will and pleasure. These

functionaries were at first known as "stipendiary magistrates" but from 1853 until their abolition under the Irish Free State as "resident magistrates".

At no period in history would the office of Justice of the Peace rank very high in a popularity poll. It would be going too far to stigmatize them all as petty tyrants but in general, at all times, the office was open to charges of corruption, irresponsibility and oppression. In a well remembered passage Shakespeare expresses a point of view that would be enthusiastically endorsed by the Irish.

LEAR: Look with thine ears: see how yond' Justice rails upon yon simple thief. Hark in thine ear, change places, and handy-dandy, which is the Justice, which is the thief? Thou has seen a farmer's dog bark at a beggar?
GLOUCESTER: Ay sir.
LEAR: And the creature run from the cur? There thou mightst behold the great image of authority; a dog's obeyed in office.
Thou rascal beadle, hold thy bloody hand!

In Ireland it was indeed rare for them to withhold their bloody hands, and this for two good reasons. In the first place their continuance in office depended on their carrying out the set policy of Dublin Castle, and secondly they were invariably judges either in their own causes or in those involving the interests of the class they represented.

For instance, in the eighteenth century the enforcement of the repressive Penal Laws was almost exclusively within their domain. In the nineteenth, most of their criminal work involved dealing with agrarian offences, game laws, poaching, affrays with the authorities and the like, while on the civil side they were mainly concerned with the pronouncement and enforcement of eviction orders against a tenantry which was legally defenceless.

To all intents and purposes the magistrate's court was the only tribunal exercising jurisdiction over the mass of the people. For the one case which came before a court presided over by a Judge trained in the law, ninety-nine came before Justices whose ignorance was only exceeded by their bias and from whose decisions there was effectively no redress. In this way, cases literally involving life and death were decided summarily and arbitrarily. Criminally, there was even power of transportation, but more terrible still were the effects of indiscriminate eviction orders which in one session alone, as in Glenveagh, involved thousands, and condemned hundreds of men, women and children to death from starvation and exposure. In cases relating to the privileges of the landowners absolutely no consideration whatsover could be invoked for the defendant; in all other cases his fate, irrespective of the evidence, depended entirely on his standing with the landlord or his agent.

In a recently published monograph on the operation of landlordism in the County of Donegal, Francis Gallagher cites an illuminating extract from a Government Blue Book of 1886, which gives the statistics of the magistracy in that year: Of the 132 Magistrates, 114 were Protestants and 18 Catholics. These figures included 80 landlords, 25 land-agents, 5 retired officers and 6 lawyers, of whom two were non-practising solicitors.

At all times after its creation the magistrates had power to call in the aid of the Royal Irish Constabulary, a para-military force, the senior members of which were themselves Justices. If this quasi-civil arm was deemed by the Justice to be insufficient then by simply reading the Riot Act he could call in the military.

This Act, which at first applied only to Ireland, was passed in 1787 and made permanent in 1800. It provided that where twelve or more were riotously and tumultuously assembled, the Justice should with a loud voice command silence and make proclamation in these words, or to like effect:

"Our Sovereign Lady the Queen chargeth and commandeth all persons being assembled immediately to disperse themselves, and peacefully to depart to their habitations, or to their lawful business upon the pains contained in the Act made in the twenty-

125

seventh year of King George the Third, to prevent tumultuous risings and assemblies."

The "pains" were that if silence were broken during the proclamation, or if the parties did not disperse within the hour, then they should be adjudged felons and suffer death as in cases of felony without benefit of clergy.

A merciful reform of Queen Victoria in 1842 altered the death penalty to merely transportation for life, or for not less than fifteen years, or imprisonment for three years. In 1860 the good lady became quite sentimental and substituted penal servitude for the transportation.

This Act supplied a weapon in the hands of the magistrates of which they were not slow to avail themselves. It was difficult to hold them liable for its misuse because the definition of "riotous and tumultuous" depended rather on the Justices' personal views than on any canon of legal construction. All over the country, therefore, peaceable assemblies were provoked by the authorities into becoming riotous mobs purely to warrant their dispersal at bayonet point and with bloodshed. Very often the same power was used at evictions which, as will be seen, frequently developed into regular small-scale battles with sometimes heavy casualties. During most of the last century, however, it was not even necessary to read the Riot Act. This was because of a succession of Coercion, and Crimes Acts, under which the liberty of the subjects was either abridged or completely abrogated, and whole districts, even counties, declared to be "proclaimed" areas by the Lord Lieutenant, thereby enabling the magistrates and the police summarily to arrest, punish and otherwise act illegally and with absolute impunity.

Yet another protection was afforded by the Castle to irresponsible incumbents of the magistrates' Bench. This was the practice of passing Acts of Indemnity, either ad hoc or generally to cover illegalities or other civil or criminal wrongs perpetuated by the Justices. The most notorious beneficiary of this indulgence by the Government was a gentleman called Thomas Judkin FitzGerald whose name is approbrious in the County of Tipperary to this day.

The behaviour of the Tipperary magistracy in the persecution of Nicholas Sheehy will be recalled. By a coincidence the town of Clonmel, in which Father Sheehy was judicially murdered, was also the scene of FitzGerald's atrocious operations. It was his boast that he "would flog every suspect until he told the truth" and in this context "suspect" was a term of art designed to embrace everyone against whom he had a grudge. One of his victims was a harmless schoolteacher named Wright against whom no possible grounds of suspicion existed. This unfortunate heard that FitzGerald was on his trail and, conscious of his innocence, he called upon him. The magistrate immediately had him seized and searched. The search discovered a note in the French language which the erudite inquisitor immediately considered, or affected to believe, was proof of communication with the enemy. It was, in fact, a note of apology from a pupil for his absence.

He ordered him five hundred lashes, then to be shot, and he himself dragged him by his hair to the triangle in the square, where he was strung up, and the scourging began with a cat-o'-nine tails which had been dipped in brine. After fifty lashes, at which stage Wright's entrails were exposed, an officer in charge of a military detachment came up to end the torture, but FitzGerald ordered another hundred lashes and had the unconscious Wright thrown on a pallet of dirty straw in the gaol, without medical attendance. Here he remained for days; somehow his fellow prisoners kept him alive and, amazingly, he recovered.

Wright brought an action in the King's Bench, and his innocence, even at a time when to be suspected of disloyalty was to be guilty of treason, was so clear that he was awarded £500 damages. Previously an Act of Indemnity had been passed protecting magistrates against their acts in cases of suspected treason. As there was no suspicion at all in this case the Act did not apply, so a further Act to indemnify FitzGerald was passed and Wright was deprived of his award.

On another occasion in the same county, when Judkin
FitzGerald was engaged in having another man flogged to
death, the victim's life was saved by the fortuitous appearance of General Sir John Moore, who threatened to have the
magistrate court-martialled and shot. This was the same John
Moore who was to die gloriously at Corunna; in that he
differed from FitzGerald who died in his bed having been
rewarded by a baronetcy for his services, which were said to
have been inscribed indelibly on the backs of his countrymen. The baronetcy, however, died out in circumstances
which vindicated the superstitious. His son died violently, his
grandson tied a stone around his neck and drowned himself
in the River Suir, while his great-grandson, the last of the
line, accidentally strangled himself when showing his play-
mates how his forebear used to hang the rebels.

As will have been gathered, the system of peace enforcement in Ireland was, to say the least of it, haphazard. It was
all very well having a pliant magistracy, but if there was no
machinery effectively to enforce its decrees and orders, it
could be compared to a gun firing blank cartridges. Robert
Peel, when Chief Secretary for Ireland, was alive to this
defect in the administration and in the second decade of the
century set about remedying it. The result was the Royal
Irish Constabulary.

It is not generally appreciated that this body antedated
its English counterpart by some fifteen years, nor that the
expression "Peelers" originated not in London, but in Dublin. Counterpart is perhaps inaccurate to describe the English
vis-à-vis the Irish force. The latter was semi-military, well-
drilled and well armed, and from its inception designed as
much to work in aid of the soldiery as the civil arm.

It was dispersed in a network which covered every town,
village and strategic point in the country, and was housed in
buildings properly called barracks, for that is what they were.
It was not without significance that in the years preceding
nineteen twenty-one both the Irish and English appreciated
the importance of this body, the former by their successful

efforts to paralyse it, and the latter in their equally strenuous efforts to strengthen it by assimilating in it the Black and Tans and the Auxiliaries, who were euphemistically known as police cadets.

Mention at this point should also be made of the Court officials who, above all, were held in the greatest odium by all classes of society. These were the process servers who were charged with the not very enviable task of serving ejectment processes, writs, execution orders and similar unpopular documents. As they were almost invariably also employed by the Sheriff to execute, as his bailiffs, the decrees of the Courts they came to be known as "bailiffs" when acting in either capacity.

It passes understanding how in the country parts of Ireland anyone could be induced to take on this job. Recruited as they were from the very class who most suffered from their visitations, they were regarded as renegades, and were considered to be perhaps one degree less reprehensible than the informers, whose ranks they not infrequently joined. In extreme cases they were murdered. They were often badly beaten, or thrown into manure heaps, and the commonest hazard of all was to be forced to eat the document they were attempting to serve. A process from the magistrate's court would not greatly tax the official's digestion, but a High Court Writ, consisting of several folio pages, was a more formidable repast.

The Galway case of Sharper v. Blake illustrates well some typical difficulties which beset the paths of these servants of the law in the execution of their duties. In that case Counsel for the Plaintiffs moved the Court on the affidavit of a process server who, having given a hair-raising account of his adventures and escapes in negotiating the demesne of the Defendant, continued:

"And, this deponent further saith, that on arriving at the house of the said Defendant, situate in the County of Galway aforesaid, for the purpose of personally serving him with the said writ, I, the said deponent, knocked three times on the hall door, but could not obtain admittance; whereupon this deponent was proceeding to knock a fourth time, when a man, to this deponent unknown, holding in his hand a musket or blunderbuss, loaded with balls or slugs, as this deponent has since heard, and, verily believes, appeared at one of the upper windows of the said house, and presenting said musket or blunderbuss at this deponent, threatened that if this deponent did not instantly retire, he would send this deponent's soul to Hell, which this deponent verily believes he would have done had not this deponent precipitately escaped."

It should also be adverted to that on some estates, and this applied particularly in the West, relations between landlord and tenant were often quite good. Where this happy situation prevailed they regarded themselves as being members of a family bound together for mutual protection, rather on the lines of the ancient Irish septs. On such estates the process server's lot was not one that any prudent life assurance company would regard with enthusiasm, as both the landlord and his tenantry united against the common foe, with the connivance of the Sheriff himself. This personage was often a relative of the judgement debtor, or had been bribed, as witness a letter, fortunately preserved, from the under-Sheriff of Mayo to the Defendant's wife, acknowledging the receipt of a bribe of two bullocks:

"Dear Madam,
    I have by this post received the two writs, as expected, from Dublin. I settled the execution against your husband. I received the two bullocks, but as cattle are down there is a balance due.
A Dublin wine merchant has just handed me an execution for £617, and insists on accompanying me to your place. I have, therefore, named Wednesday, on which day you will please have the doors closed against us. As the Plaintiff may again be officious I would recommend his being *ducked* when returning; and a city bailiff, whom you will know by his having a scorbutic face, and a yellow waistcoat, should, for many reasons, be corrected. Pray take care the boys don't go too far, as manslaughter, under the late Act, is now a transportable felony. Tell your uncle Ulick I have returned *non est inventus* (cannot be found) to his last three execution orders, but *he must not show*. After we return *nulla bona* on Wednesday next, I will come out and arrange matters.
    Believe me, my dear Madam, truly yours, . . ."

130

Such amity between landlord and tenantry, however, was anything but usual. Throughout the last century the reality was very different, and such landlords as lived on their estates, and their agents, were bitter enemies of the people in an implacable warfare. One or two examples of the lengths to which both attackers and defenders were prepared to go, in the battles which were commonplace in every county, will give some idea of how bitterly the land war was waged.

One famous example was the resistance to eviction of the Widow Boyle of Upper Dore, in the Rosses of Donegal. This woman with her young family lived on the notorious Hill estate, and in pursuance of what was known as an "improvement policy" was duly served with an eviction order. On the morning the order was to be executed, some hundreds of neighbours turned up, from which company two men, Dominick Rogers and Owen Boyle, as well as two relatives of the Widow, Mary Boyle and Kate O'Donnell, were selected to constitute the garrison. The women's pricipal function was to maintain a continuous supply of scalding hot thin porridge, or stirabout, which was a highly effective defensive weapon. The little cottage was then fortified with a large quantity of heavy bog-wood and shuttered, bolted and barred. Thus prepared, the occupants awaited developments which were not long in coming to a head.

In less than an hour the sound of marching feet and military commands announced the arrival of the Resident Magistrate, Thomas W. French, the land-agent, Lieutenant Colonel Doppins, a medical doctor, a District Inspector at the head of a force of about a hundred armed police, the Sheriff's bailiffs and, most important of all, a detachment of "emergency men" or temporary bailiffs specially sworn in for the occasion, who could be described as the storm troops of the party.

When this array was halted and deployed around the widow's cottage the Magistrate formally demanded possession in the name of the Law, and received the answer he expected—complete silence. Operations then began by an emergency man smashing a hole in the door with a crow-bar. Through this aperture he immediately received a pot full of boiling stirabout in the face, and the doctor had a scream-ing patient on his hands.

After this preliminary skirmish the bailiffs held a council of war, as a result of which one of them surreptitiously went around to the windowless gable and began to undermine the foundations with his crow-bar. He could not, of course, be seen by the beleaguered, and would probably have brought down the wall were it not for the warning shouts of the people outside. On hearing them, Manus Boyle placed a ladder against the inner gable wall and broke a hole in the thatched roof. His companion climbed up with a large boulder which he dropped on the back of the industrious bailiff, who in turn was carried away to the doctor.

This sparked off the excited crowd who now began to rain missiles on the bailiffs. The Colonel complained to the In-spector that the police were not protecting his men. He, in turn, remonstrated with the parish priest who was present and who replied that he would not interfere with a woman's right to defend her home.

The attack was resumed, and this time an emergency man succeeded in getting up on the roof with the intention of breaking through in that way. Again the crowd shouted to the besieged who, when they saw the roof sag under the man's weight, obtained a long bog-spear. This is a really lethal instrument, rather like a lance or pike, and as sharp as a razor. One of them stood on the kitchen table and lunged with it through the thatch, impaling the invader who fell off in agony, supplying yet another patient to the over-worked medico.

Things had now begun to become really serious, and the Resident Magistrate decided to treat the crowd as accessories because of their warnings. He called for silence and read the Riot Act to them. Having done so the police were drawn up and ordered to load their rifles and prepare to fire on the people. This, incidentally, was quite illegal until an hour had expired from the reading of the Act, unless the constabulary were placed in peril of their lives, and it occasioned the most dramatic incident of that eventful morning.

A young constable named Thomas Haughrey stepped out of the ranks and saluted his officer, District Inspector Winder. He informed him that he would never be a party to firing on any unarmed people, much less his own country-men. He then unslung his rifle and equipment and threw them on the ground, for which action he was seized and placed under arrest. On later resigning from the Royal Irish Constabulary he was released and emigrated to the United States.

This contretemps caused a lull in the hostilities during which a parley was held between the Inspector and the priest, Canon McFadden. The latter agreed to induce the inmates of the house to surrender if the officer would use his influence to mitigate their punishment. On this undertaking the garrison of three women and two men emerged with their battle honours intact.

In the same month and district a similar eviction order was executed at the cottage of another widow, Mrs. Mary Bonner. After several bailiffs were more or less seriously in-jured, and when the four walls were breached and the roof had collapsed, an assault was made with fixed bayonets, which carried the citadel. This time all the defenders, four women and one man, were casualties, the man and one of the women being dragged unconscious from the debris.

In the far South the story was the same, and A. M. Sullivan describes a case in which he was involved as counsel as being the best organized defence in his experience. This eviction was ordered to take place at a townland called Watergrass Hill in the County Cork, and the usual force of horse and foot set forth from Fermoy. The defenders had, however, so directed their force that the march was impeded en route long before the main lines of defence were reached, by lines of girls lying on the roadway. The removal and disposal of these obstructions took several hours, and when at length

133

the farmhouse was reached a moat had been dug around it. This was fed from an adjoining stream and with the contents of a considerable manure heap. The house itself stood on a steepish hill. The lower story, windows and doors, were securely barricaded, while in the upper was a supply of boulders and small stones, as well as unlimited quantities of meal for making the deadly, scalding stirabout.

The bailiffs, understandably, did not venture too near to stirabout range, but even at a distance were subjected to a fusillade of stones. Their leader then demanded possession from afar, whereupon the farm owner's solicitor informed him that the demand was illegal, not having been made on the premises. This preliminary law point was considered and overruled and the emergency men returned to the assault.

Under fire they managed to erect at the door a wooden support from which they slung a heavy log which acted as a battering ram. The general order to advance was then given and the armed forces of the Royal Irish Constabulary began their ascent of the hill. The advance came to a sudden halt because the garrison in the upper story now brought their heavy artillery to bear. For this purpose they had engaged the services of the champion weight thrower of the county to discharge from the windows huge boulders too heavy for an ordinary man to lift. These were sent bounding down the hill, among the ranks of the attackers who were scattered and re-scattered every time they re-formed. Even when it appeared that ammunition was giving out, and that the next assault must succeed, the champion got the brain wave of using large rocks forming part of the fortress structure. These he prised loose and the forces of the law, to their astonishment and dismay, found themselves being bombarded with the actual house itself. This improvised ammunition eventually ran out, of course, and by nightfall when both the defenders and their means of defence were exhausted the place was rushed and taken.

Most evictees did not put up such spirited resistances. For the most part they were driven in despair from their cottages, which were demolished, and the tenants and their families were faced with the choice of starvation on the roads, or the lingering heartbreak of the workhouse. There was always, of course, the emigrant ship and exile.

It can be seen that, by and large, the genial and beloved R.M. presiding avuncularly over the zany disputes of the feckless but engaging natives was more a pleasant conceit of Mesdames Somerville and Ross than a paradigm of the reality. Nowhere in the pages of these excellent ladies will one find a disturbing reference to the evictions, sentences, fines, whippings and petty tyrannies practised by the Magistracy on a people from whom it differed in spirit and in sympathy. Again, it must be repeated, no generalization is true of Ireland. Just as there were good landlords so there were magistrates who, if falling short of the benevolence of the R.M. of Somerville and Ross, at least had a sense of duty, and *Some Reminiscences of an Irish R.M.* was written about the time when such were less uncommon than at any previous period.

This was also the period when the *ancien régime* of the Justices' Bench was leavened, or rather adulterated, by a widespread enrolment of new magistrates which, in an inimitable way, made a contribution to maladministration that amounted to high genius. It could now be said of the J.P.'s bench that if the old magistrates tortured the Spirit of Justice, this new creation spat in her eye. They were drawn from that class of petty Irish politician which, mushroom-like, springs up in any soil which has been well manured with pseudo-patriotic sentiment. Immediately known as "Morley Magistrates" from the Chief Secretary who appointed them, they were selected by Irish Members of Parliament whose support was so important to the Liberal Government of the day.

Their claim to judicial appointment, it is hardly necessary to say, was founded solely but securely on interest with the sitting member. This could be exploited either by an uncomfortable intimate knowledge of the legislator's private life, or an influence in local affairs that could command votes. In this way gombeen men and their ilk became aspirants to a social grandeur on the bench of a Court in which their fathers had probably appeared in the dock.

The result can hardly be said to have poisoned the wells of a form of Justice which had been pretty thoroughly polluted already but, by adding to the magistracy a different conception of venality, turned the solemnities of injustice into a sort of opéra bouffe. At least it can be said that from the time these dogs in office were unleashed upon the community, their barkings and antics on the bench invested the Court with an entertainment value which hitherto had been notably absent from its proceedings. It is from this time that the origins of those judicial aberrations which have become famous in song and story, and have made Justices' Justice proverbial, can be dated.

In every sense of the word the most rewarding field in which they exercised jurisdiction was in the administration and interpretation of the licencing laws, and indeed this was a branch of jurisprudence to which their talents were pre-eminently suited. The task of the unfortunate condemned to negotiate the Minoan maze was simple compared to that of the practitioner trying to find his way through the Irish Licencing Laws. It is, in a way, a great tribute to the godlike ingenuity of man that the superficially simple transaction of buying and selling a drink could be hedged in with so many statutes, rules, regulations, prohibitions, exceptions, penalties, by-laws and mumbo-jumbo generally as to defeat the understanding of the most experienced jurist. When to this hotch-potch of legal confusion were added the spices of an unprincipled bench, and an array of mendacious witnesses, it will be appreciated that while a licencing case could be complicated it was seldom dull.

Many are the tales that have come down of the mighty deeds and brilliant coups that were accomplished both in and out of the witness box, in frustrating the knavish tricks of the authorities in their attempts to abridge the inalienable right of an Irishman to have a drink at any hour of the day or night he feels like it. One of the most outrageous took place in that far famed nursery of legal ingenuity, County Kerry.

In this particular prosecution the evidence of the sergeant was that he knocked at the pub door several times before being admitted. He had already seen several men drinking on the premises at least two hours after closing time. There were dirty glasses on the counter, and a strong smell of tobacco smoke. There was also a case against the publican who, in his statement, had denied that there had been anyone present after hours, that he himself was a heavy pipe smoker, and that he intended to clean out the place in the morning. The solicitor for the publican and the alleged delinquents then took up the running:

SOLICITOR: I put it to you that the pub was shuttered, and locked, and no light showing when you arrived at it?

SERGEANT: That is so.

SOLICITOR: How then do you say you were able to see these men drinking at the end of the bar?

SERGEANT: Because I saw them through the flap of the letter-box.

SOLICITOR: How could you, if it was dark?

SERGEANT: There was a candle, and I know each of them and I saw each of them by the light of the candle.

SOLICITOR: And you lifted the flap of the letter-box to look in through it?

SERGEANT: That is right.

SOLICITOR: You swear that on your oath?

SERGEANT: Of course I do.

At this point a great hugger-mugger took place between the licensee and his solicitor, who then turned to the bench and said: "May it please your worship, my client has just acquainted me with a most important, and I may say, grave piece of information. He tells me that, in fact, there is no letter-box at all on the door of his public house.

This announcement created a furore, and when the dust cleared it was decided that one and all should there and then inspect the premises. The Court was adjourned and, as the solicitor had said, there was no letter-box on the door nor sign of one ever having been on it. Furthermore, it was clearly a door which had been in use for years.

On resumption, the case was dismissed and the unfortunate sergeant was informed that if the Court had the power it would have no compunction in sending him to jail for perjury. As it was, a strong report would be sent to his superiors. This was done, and although his superiors knew him to be honest, and that there was something fishy about the whole thing, for his own good they transferred him to a distant part of the country.

It may be added that the publican had omitted to point out that he and his friends had substituted the door from one of his outhouses for the original which, with its letter-box, made excellent kindling when broken up.

There is also recorded in Petty Sessions annals a similar prosecution, but with a very dissimilar result, in which the rout of the publican and his advisers was complete. The defending solicitor's name was not Dan O'Shaughnessy, but that is as good an identification as any for the purposes of the case. He was a performer of some renown, particularly on what could be called the licencing side of the court, and as the young officer who had conducted the raid was an untried fledgling success for temperance appeared unlikely.

In cross-examination Mr. O'Shaughnessy was impressive, awe-inspiring, and faintly satirical:

— You did not, in fact, actually apprehend anyone on the premises?
— I did not, because they got out the back before I got in.
— Did you see them going out?
— No, but they couldn't have gone the other way.
— I suggest you saw no one at all on the premises?
— I did not, but I heard them.
— And is it your sworn evidence that you could identify each of these men by their voices?
— It is, and I'll swear it again.
— Can you remember what they said to each other?
— I can.

— Come on then, and tell the Court.

— I prefer not to answer, Mr. O'Shaughnessy.

— I insist on an answer, and kindly remember where you are, sir.

— Oh, very well, if that's the way of it. I heard John O'Shea there say to Tom Lyons "It's the bloody Police that's in it," and then Lyons said "Ah! sure what the hell about it; if we're caught itself sure won't you get us out of it, Mister O'Shaughnessy."

A battle-scarred warrior like Dan should have had more sense than to press a reluctant policeman, for even if he did not know the answer, his reputation for omniscience depended upon his saying something. An excellent example of this was when a judge incautiously said to a sergeant witness who had given some startling evidence: "It reminds me of an observation of Tacitus, *Omne ignotum pro magnifico* (Everything unknown is wonderful)", to receive the reply: "Your lordship has took the words out of my mouth."

It was at the licencing sessions, and in the applications for public house licences, that the flower of the bench was seen in its fullest bloom. In such cases every comfort, aid and maintenance would be afforded to the learned J.P.s by the applicant, and if an occasional *douceur* was given, well the Irish are a generous race. The Law Reports are replete with decisions of the superior courts to which the infuriated authorities were forced to have recourse in order to reverse the fantasies of the learned justices.

These fantasies, for they were nothing else, by their frequency also gave rise to the most extraordinary legal misapprehensions. To this day, for example, it is an article of faith in the countryside that if some shebeen on top of a mountain opens up on one day in the year and sells one bottle of stout, the requirements of conducting a bona fide trade during the twelve months preceding the application are satisfied. It is difficult to blame the people for this belief because suitably sweetened magistrates granted innumerable renewals on no stronger evidence of trading.

The bona fide traveller himself, whoever *he* was, was also a gentleman who figured prominently in the juristic deliberations of the bench. The law prescribed a three-mile limit

139

within which the wayfarer's right to freedom from thirst was inhibited. This led to the interesting sight on a Sunday morning of a bus bringing the inhabitants of village A to the nearest public house in village B, where the same bus picked up the citizens of B, who were similarly bound for A. It had less happy results around the cities where "doin' the bona fides" by car after the pubs closed at night became a national pastime which was not abolished until 1961. This nonsense was, naturally, meat and drink to the Justices of the Peace who ascribed to the expression "bona fide" recondite and conflicting implications which the most erudite scholar could be forgiven for not suspecting.

The lamentable reign of the Petty Sessions bench came to an end with the setting up of the Provisional Government of the Irish Free State after the Treaty of 1922. In the years preceding that event legal chaos and anarchy had prevailed throughout the country. In fact, from 1919 the only courts which exercised effective jurisdiction were those set up by what was then the illegal legislature of Ireland, Dail Eireann.

The Dail itself came into existence in a manner that could only have happened in Ireland—as a result of its members being elected to the House of Commons in a British election. This was the famous 1918 "Hang the Kaiser" election. For the first time the Sinn Fein party had an opportunity to come before the Irish electorate and it swept the country, annihilating in the process the old Irish Nationalist party which was wiped off the political map.

The Sinn Fein candidates were pledged not to sit in Westminster. Instead, such as were not in jail met in the Mansion House in Dublin, the official headquarters of the Lord Mayor, and declared themselves the first Dail Eireann or parliament of the Irish people. Hostilities with the Crown forces were under way, although not yet on the scale of the next two years.

Despite this, they set up departments of state, including a Ministry of Justice charged *inter alia* with setting up law courts, which was done. These courts were known to the people as the Republican Courts, and were the tribunals to which the people resorted. They had their own police. Their judgements were obeyed and their decrees, in so far as could be, executed. Most of the members of these courts were lawyers, and one of them, Cahir Davitt, was to become President of the High Court, the second judicial office in the country.

Petty Sessions now became a dead letter, and after a while did not go through the formality of sitting at all. The superior courts from the County Court upwards were rendered practically impotent, and it has happened that a High Court Judge, or a Lord Justice, would arrive at an Assize town where, in full regalia and attended by the High Sheriff and other dignitaries, together with a detachment of the military, he would proceed in state to the Courthouse. When he took his place on the bench he would find himself presiding over a court empty except for his Registrar, some Court officials and a few policemen. The Registrar would then inquire if there were any applications to the Court, and on receiving no reply from the vacuum would declare the sessions closed; his lordship took the earliest train back to Dublin.

While these impressive proceedings were taking place, the Republican court down the road was in the course of transacting its heavy business, with impartiality and despatch. For that matter numerous cases were successfully brought by parties aggrieved by the illegal actions of alleged Republican sympathizers who thought that they could interfere with the rights and property of others with impunity. Their own courts drastically showed them that they were in error.

This strangulation of administration was more than the British Government could stomach, and in 1920 its reply was to pass what was euphemistically and optimistically known as The Restoration of Order (Ireland) Act. Even Hitler at his most inventive never thought up anything more drastic; among its provisions it gave capital powers to magistrates, and authorized naval and military officers to set up tribunals vested also with capital jurisdiction. It made provision for regulations to declare hours of curfew, domiciliary raids,

141

arrest without warrant, and all kinds of illegal processes, most of which were also clothed with the ultimate sanction of the death penalty. To give teeth and effect to these ordinances, Hamar Greenwood supplied the Black and Tans and the Auxiliaries, and the stage was set.

Well could it be said with Macduff, "Confusion now hath made his masterpiece, most sacrilegious murder hath broke ope. . . ."

The state of the law was indeed a masterpiece of confusion. Under the R.O. (I) Act martial law was declared over most of the country, and at one time no fewer than seven Southern counties were placed under its sway. There were three jurisdictions attempting to function in the country, all of them mutually antagonistic: the ordinary courts, the military tribunals and the Republican courts. Actually, in consonance with the dictum that "martial law is no law" the High Court, with great courage, reprimanded the General Officer Commanding in Limerick and peremptorily ordered a writ of *habeas corpus* to be served on him.

At last the Treaty was signed, and when midnight struck on December 6 1922 it sounded the death-knell of the office of Justice and Keeper of the Peace in Ireland.

In view of the strictures which down the years have been passed on the corruption, oppression and sycophancy of so many incumbents of that office, when recording its demise it would be unfair not to record at least one instance when a Justice displayed his pride and independence in a letter which is a miracle of such sustained and withering contempt as to rank it with Johnson's letter to Lord Chesterfield:

*To the Right Honourable John Earl of Clare,*
*Lord High Chancellor of Ireland*
My Lord,
  With surprise and sorrow I received a letter signed 'J. Dwyer' informing me that your Lordship was pleased to suspend me in the Commission of the Peace for the Counties of Leitram and Roscommon. I say 'with surprise', as I am not conscious of any fault to warrant such a proceeding on the part of your Lordship.

I add 'with sorrow' for, low as the appointment is—and low in-deed it must be, depending upon the caprice of any individual—yet, as it afforded me the power to protect innocence and counter-act tyranny, I part from it with regret.

Your Lordship loves not the Constitution with more zeal than I do; it has been the theme of my continual panegyrics, nor shall the unkind treatment I experience at your Lordship's hands tend to demoralize my opinions; quite the reverse. It is to me an addi-tional proof of my aristocratic creed 'that there is in men of mean descent an innate ignobility which no titles or honours can eradi-cate.' It is not, my Lord, in the radiance of the royal sunbeam to give to the mushroom the fragrance of the rose; and when we look to a new man for the bland and golden dignity of manners which mark the genuine noblesse, we too often find a pinchbeck petu-lance substituted in its stead. When I waited on your Lordship with a letter from the Governor of the County in which my family resides, with an affected hauteur, which ill becomes the man of yesterday, you turned on your heel, and refused me an opportunity of justifying my conduct. Had your Lordship, like your father, been destined for the Popish priesthood, you would have had the benefit of a St. Omer's education, and in conse-quence know more decency and good manners; but probably a giddy head is turned by looking down from a pinnacle to which a fortunate combination of circumstances has raised it. Yet, ele-vated as your Lordship is, it never appeared to me that when I heard your Lordship's voice, 'an Angel spoke'.

Your *tout ensemble* has rather recalled to my fancy the figure of a sweep who, climbing through dirt, pops out his sooty-coloured face and, with a shrill voice, proclaims his high situation to the world. It has been asserted by your Lordship that I took bail for several persons under the denomination of 'defenders', nothing more being specified in the committal, and your Lord-ship is the most competent Judge, whether that is sufficient to detain his Majesty's subjects. It has been represented that one of the parties houghed a cow, and hung a threatening notice on one of her horns. Had he houghed your Lordship and hung a threaten-ing notice on one of your horns, under the same committal I would have acted in the same manner. I cannot dismiss this letter without a comment on the impertinence of your Lordship's ser-vant, but that is easily accounted for by recollecting 'that man is an imitative animal', and perhaps I attribute to impoliteness a conduct which might, with more propriety, be attributed to fear; but so high is my respect for official situation that, though it rained horsewhips, far be it from me to think of laying one of them on the hem of your Lordship's garment.

I am, my Lord, with sincerity to my enemies, and respect to myself,                                          G. N. REYNOLDS.

Obviously, not all magistrates were tarred with the same brush, and there were others who attempted to discharge their duties with humanity and honesty. It is fitting that this magnificent letter be rescued from undeserved oblivion to stand as their memorial.

On the passing of the Constitution Act of 1922 to which the Treaty was scheduled, a legal vacuum was created. The British forces had departed with their military courts, the old magistracy was *functus officio*, and there were no republican courts. There was no tribunal exercising a summary jurisdiction, and legal cynics and disgruntled litigants have frequently said that this happy circumstance presented the Government with a god-sent opportunity not to supply one. It did supply one, however, and so came into existence the District Court presided over by District Justices.

Whatever its failings the new dispensation was immediately seen to be a vast improvement on the old. District Justices must have been practising barristers or solicitors for at least six years before appointment; their jurisdiction is much wider than that of their predecessors, being almost comparable to that of the English County Court; and above all, they are not removable before retiring age, except by reason of mental or physical infirmity or misconduct, and then only by resolution passed on a two-thirds majority of both the Dail and the Senate.

In this way their office partakes of many of the incidents of a judgeship and confers on them an independence from interference by the executive which was a badly needed reform. Indeed, this very independence, so admirable in many ways, has frequently bred an attitude of majestic detachment from a slavish deference to legal principles which so constrains the proceedings in the superior courts. In pursuance of this unfettered interpretation of justice, where a discretion is conferred on the Justice it will generally be exercised with reference to his personal prejudices rather than to the facts of the case.

The most notorious illustration of capriciousness of this

sort was afforded by a District Justice who announced that he would impose a jail sentence on all whom he convicted of being incapable because of drink, of exercising effective control over motor cars driven in a certain town. When it was pointed out to him that the Act conferred a discretion to impose either a fine or imprisonment, dependent presumably on the presence or absence of mitigating circumstances or the gravity of the offence, he replied that in every case under the section he would exercise the discretion of sending the accused to jail. The result, of course, was that such decisions were invariably appealed, and almost invariably either reversed or varied. This afforded excellent business for the legal profession on Circuit even if it was not quite so financially profitable for the unfortunate clients.

The decisions of another Justice in another area are still spoken of with awe as they bore on the face of them all the indicia of being pronounced by a religious maniac, which in fact they were. When an English boy was found kissing an Irish girl he was released on condition that he did not return to Ireland for twelve months. This was effectively a deportation order, which not even the Government had power to make. One feels, however, that the boy had already decided to spend his next holiday on the continent.

This same Justice was also convinced that ballroom dancing was a cunning and subtle contrivance of the Devil designed primarily for the corruption of Irish maidenhood and youth. This would have been a harmless enough obsession were it not that dance hall proprietors must renew their licences each year on application to the District Court. The Justice sturdily refused to renew the licences except on condition that at least fifty per cent of the dances each night would be Irish dances.

There were two strong objections to the imposition of this judicial restriction. Firstly, it has as yet defeated the wit of man to lay down what terpsichorean gyrations will satisfy the definition of Irish dancing, and secondly it was completely illegal. Both considerations were urged upon his Worship in vain, and year after year the Circuit Court for that county had the unique distinction of being the only tribunal in which dance hall licence appeals formed a major part of the business.

Another side effect of the comparative autonomy of the summary court is the opportunity it gives the bench to avoid such hazards to mental and physical health as are attributable to over-work. One hastens to add that this observation emphatically does not apply to Dublin Justices, or many of their colleagues in the thickly populated areas, whose numbers should, in fact, be supplemented. In more far-flung parts, however, there used to be, and generally speaking is, no imminent danger of collapses from exhaustion from this cause.

One Justice, who was clearly very much alive to such dangers, and equally concerned to ward them off, dispensed summary justice in a Connaught county in the years before the last war.

This gentleman shared with some of his brethren a disdain for the conventional forms of law as expressed in the more usually accepted text-books, and on appointment equipped himself with a library which consisted of *Every Man His Own Lawyer*, and *Old Moore's Almanac*. The former he deemed more than adequate to resolve such legal controversies as were liable to arise, and the latter was important in enabling him to ensure that his sittings did not clash with the fair days within his jurisdiction. For the episode with which we are concerned this invaluable work provided further useful information.

On this occasion when his Worship took his place on the bench, the assembled solicitors were concerned to note that he was suffering from what in England is unimaginatively known as a hang-over, but in Ireland as "the shakes". This augured ill for the conduct of the day's business, which was heavy. But they need not have worried!

In a most solemn manner the Justice stood up, called for silence, and directed everyone in Court also to stand up;

146

whereupon he delivered a speech in these terms: "Gentle-men, as you are all aware, to-day marks the anniversary of the death of Marshal MacMahon, the first President of the Third French Republic, a great French soldier and, we are proud to claim, also a great Irishman. It is unnecessary for me to expatiate on the close ties which have always existed between our two great countries. Accordingly, as a mark of deference to his memory I propose to adjourn to-day's business."

Everyone then adjourned to the nearest hostelry where the jurist-historian received the congratulations of a number of solicitors who had attended the same function the previous night and were not themselves feeling too strong.

However, there is a limit even in the West of Ireland, and it was reached three weeks later when in similar circum-stances, having again consulted *Old Moore*, he adjourned the court on the anniversary of the death of Paul Kruger, first President of the Third Boer Republic. This was too much for one solicitor who had had trouble already explaining to his clients why their cases had not come to hearing. Having a sense of humour he sent an account of the proceedings to the editor of a well-known legal journal in England, as a result of which there appeared in the next issue under Items of Legal Interest:

An event unprecedented in legal history since Lord Coleridge adjourned the Queen's Bench on the death of the Duke of Wel-lington occurred last week in Mohill in the County of Leitrim, when the learned District Justice adjourned the sitting of his court as a tribute to the memory of the late Paul Kruger on the 29th anniversary of his death. We are informed that this prece-dent is unlikely to be followed by the Metropolitan Courts in London.

Despite such aberrations, the Bench of District Justices has proved itself and such failings as individuals have dis-played from time to time are fortunately attributable to the frailty of human nature, rather than the rottenness of the system it replaced. It is primarily designed to inquire into and do justice to the facts and in this, by and large, it admirably succeeds. When a legal proposition is presented to it by the advocate, the Court is not to be blamed if it has neither the time nor the equipment to inquire too closely into its validity, and in this regard it is a pity that Parliament in its wisdom has left on the Statute Books so many Acts which are either inoperable or obsolete, an omission which has from time to time had some extraordinary results.

Quite recently, in fact, two boys were hauled before the District Court for poaching rabbits in the night-time. There was no defence as they had been caught red-handed and so their solicitor pleaded guilty for them. Quite properly the Justice inquired were there any previous convictions and he was informed yes there were two, also for poaching rabbits. The following fantasy then ensued:

JUSTICE: What did I do on those occasions?

SERGEANT: On the first occasion you applied the Probation Act, and on the second you fined them ten shillings each.

JUSTICE: Oh! Is that so? Well, this time I'll teach them a good lesson. I am fining them thirty shillings each.

SOLICITOR FOR DEFENCE: You can't do that, Justice.

JUSTICE: Can I not! I have just done it.

SOLICITOR: Well you have no jurisdiction to do it. My clients are charged under an Act of George IV, The Night Poaching Act, and Section 3, which applies here, provides that on conviction for a third offence under the Act the only jurisdiction is penal servitude for not less than five years, or transportation for life.

This startling piece of legal enlightenment gave rise to a discussion as to what Irish colony would be most appropriate, and a suggestion that the delinquents be marooned on Dalkey Island was overruled. In the event, the fortunate Nimrods received the Probation Act again.

# 9

## Bench and Bar

It is important to remember that in the superior courts, including the Circuit Court, the bench and bar are members of the same profession. The function of the one is to assess the submissions on the law and the facts, and of the other to present them in a manner best calculated to serve the interests of the client for whom he is retained. This last proposition requires the qualification that no barrister is entitled to mislead the court deliberately. The object of the system is the achievement of justice, even if that laudable object is somewhat befogged betimes in the smoke of battle. On the whole, however, the system works.

There have always been in the layman's mind a number of misconceptions as to the privileges and duties of counsel, vis-à-vis the Court, and in consulting his client's interests. The answers to them can best be epitomized by saying that he is entitled to do everything for his client which the client could do for himself had he the requisite training. He is in no circumstances entitled deliberately to mislead the Court. For instance, he is not entitled to rely on an Act which he knows is repealed, or cite a case which has been overruled. He can, however, having presented the law attempt to place on it the complexion most favourable to his case.

Again, barristers are often asked "how can you defend a man whom you know to be guilty!" The answer is that the question of guilt is a matter for the judge and jury alone, and that if this were to be predetermined by a barrister it would exclude great numbers charged with unpopular crimes from the protection of the law. At the same time, when a prisoner has confessed to his counsel the latter cannot put him in the witness-box to perjure himself, nor can he cross-examine the prosecution witnesses to show that any of them, or someone else, was the perpetrator. It was this very transgression in Courvoisier's murder trial that finished the career of Phillips at the Bar. What counsel can do and, short of pleading guilty, must do, is put the prosecution upon the strictest proof of his client's guilt.

The object of a criminal trial is not to determine the innocence of the accused but his guilt, and the onus of proof is fairly and squarely on the prosecution. Counsel is entitled, whatever his personal knowledge, to show in cross-examination that this onus has not been discharged and if it has not been to demand an acquittal.

This principle was well expressed by F. E. Smith when, in defending Ethel Le Neve, whom he did not call to give evidence, for complicity in the Crippen murder, he said to the jury "it is not, never was, and, please God, never will be, the law, that an accused person be called on to give an explanation of his conduct, when no evidence of guilt has been adduced." A quarter of a century later in the successful appeal by Woolmington against conviction for murder, the court itself referred to the presumption of the innocence of the accused as "the golden thread" which ran through the administration of justice.

It is as well to point out that the duty of counsel to the court does not end at refraining from misleading it, it goes as far as not permitting it to be misled. For example, if a barrister is present and hears the court acceding to a proposition in law which he knows to be erroneous, such as a submission based on a repealed enactment, he is bound to intervene, even if he is not engaged in the case. It must be added that in no circumstances is his personal opinion relevant, and to express it in regard to the truth or falsity of his client's case would be visited with a severe reprimand, if not worse.

With, therefore, the qualification of never acting *mala fide*, the client's interests are—or should be—paramount to any other consideration whatsoever, and that means even his own, his family's or society itself. Curran was displaying the high traditions of the Irish Bar when, defending Oliver Bond for high treason in Green Street, he faced the bayonets of the soldiers who threatened him and defied them. "You may assassinate, but you will not intimidate me."

Fortunately, it is rare for a barrister to be in bodily peril, but it is not by any means unusual for him to be called on to act in cases which can seriously react upon his own affairs. In such cases his duty is clear. This duty necessarily entails his assertion of the independence of his profession, for just as that of the judiciary is the best guarantee of impartial justice so is the independence of the Bar the safeguard of the subject in the assertion of his rights. This can often lead to conflict with the Judges, for even the best are human and can go off the rails, and in the last century when the integrity of both bench and bar was not always above suspicion the passages were fiery indeed.

The Irish Bar at all periods was noted for its wit, and most of the anecdotes that have come down to us have as their point the discomfiture of the Judge. This is probably because everyone has an anarchistic streak which rejoices in the deflation of authority. Not infrequently, however, authority scores. The late Judge Gleeson when presiding over a criminal trial in County Donegal persistently warned the solicitor for the prisoner about his cross-examination of the prosecution witnesses. At length this gentleman protested: "I have a duty to defend my client, and I must protest to your lordship against your interruptions."

His Lordship observed: "I, too, have a duty in this Court. It is to see that justice is done, and part of that duty is to protect the prisoner against the incompetence of his own advisers."

A similar judicial torpedo was unloosed by a Judge in the Dublin Circuit Court. The case at hearing was an application by a shopkeeper for compensation for a broken plate-glass window, which under Irish law is payable by the ratepayers if the breakage was malicious. At the end of the case counsel for the Dublin Corporation, resisting the claim, cited an authority from the Law Reports, and said: "I must inform your lordship that while I put this case as a true expression of the law, at the same time it is not binding on you as it is a decision of your brother, Judge Shannon, in the Circuit Court."

The Judge thanked him, remarked that he always paid the greatest deference to his brother Shannon's decisions and invited the submissions of the other side. The applicant's counsel announced that he was in a different position from his learned friend and proposed to cite a case which had been decided in the High Court by Mr. Justice Gavan Duffy, and was directly in point. This he proceeded to do, and his lordship listened attentively.

In the course of his judgement, the Judge referred to counsel's submissions somewhat in these terms: "Having heard the case which Judge Shannon decided, and to which I was referred by counsel for the Corporation, I was disposed to decide against him. Now, however, that I have read the decision of the High Court, which is binding on me, I am constrained to decide in his favour, and, accordingly, I dismiss this application with costs."

Generally, the boot is on the other foot and it is the counsel who has looked up his law for the case who, naturally, has the advantage. This was exemplified on an immortal occasion in the Exchequer Court by Robert Holmes, who was the terror of the bench although, ironically, his son became a Lord Justice in later years. It would seem that Holmes was unsuccessfully pressing a point on the learned Barons who were unanimously against him. He finally said he would be content if they would allow him to refer to a recent House of Lords decision which he felt might influence them. "No use, whatever, Mr. Holmes," replied the Chief Baron.

"Only two lines, my lord," pleaded the persistent barrister.

"Well, Mr. Holmes," observed Baron Pennefeather, "if the case is in point, and you will be as brief as all that, we might as well hear it."

Holmes thanked him, opened a recent volume of House of Lords cases and read an excerpt from an appeal case reversing a decision of the Barons, which said: "The Court of Common Pleas in Ireland is seldom right—The Court of Exchequer never."

This was the same counsel who arrived in court one day in the company of a very long-winded performer, one James Scott, Q.C. When the next case was called, Scott stood up, and said. "My lords, I beg to assure your lordships that I am so exhausted that I am quite unable to argue this case. I have been speaking for three hours in the Court of Exchequer, and I am quite tired out. I would be grateful if your lordships would permit me to retire for some refreshments."

"Certainly, Mr. Scott," said the Chief Justice, and the learned gentleman left the court.

"Ah! I see, Mr. Holmes, that you are in Court," said the Chief Justice, "we will be happy to hear you."

"Really, my lord, I am very tired too," said Mr. Holmes.

"Surely," said the Chief Justice "you have not been speaking for three hours in the Court of Exchequer! What has tired you?"

"Listening to Mr. Scott," was the reply.

These, of course, were comparatively harmless pieces of effrontery. The insolence could sometimes be deadly, and Tim Healy, K.C., who was described by Tom Kettle as "that brilliant calamity", had the deadliest tongue of all.

On one occasion Healy was appearing in a case before Mr. Justice Gibbon in circumstances which he did not relish. The circumstances were that Gibbon's son had recently been called to the Bar, a legal event which a number of solicitors celebrated by briefing him to appear for them in his father's court. It was the popular and defamatory belief that these causes would have been decided in the privacy of the judicial residence the night before they came to hearing.

This particular action was going extremely badly for Healy. The judge continuously interrupted, short-circuited his witnesses, and generally misbehaved. The atmosphere was charged with electricity when Healy submitted a proposition of law which gave rise to further adverse comment from the bench. Healy persisted until finally the Judge completely lost his temper: "Mr. Healy," he said, "I absolutely and completely fail to see your point."

"I didn't think your lordship would," said Tim with unwonted suavity. "The son is in your eyes!"

This type of remark, if insolent, stems from a sense of professional pride. There have been occasions when Judges have sat in courts empty of counsel until they have publicly made amends for some insult to a member of the Bar, which has been held by the Bar Council to be unwarranted and which called for an apology. On the other hand, when Counsel has exceeded his privileges in Court, and gratuitously insulted the Judge, the Bar Council have been equally jealous to inquire into the circumstances and deal appropriately with the offender.

In former times when political and religious passion was at its height, the rows that took place in Court were charged not merely with insolence, but with the most heartfelt bitterness. Even now, it is difficult to read, unmoved, the famous passage between Curran and Mr. Justice Robinson. This latter, one of the many Government appointees who disgraced the judicial office at the time, owed his position to his facility for producing badly written and defamatory books and pamphlets aimed at the opponents of the Government.

In a case in which Robinson decided against a legal submission of the newly called barrister, the latter said that he was unaware of having read his lordship's proposition in the law books; this opening was duly pounced on by the Judge, who said: "That may be so, but I suspect your library is not extensive."

"In that your lordship is correct," was the answer, "I am poor and my books are not numerous, but they are select. I have prepared myself for this high profession rather by the study of a few good books than by the composition of a great many bad ones. I would add that I am not ashamed of my poverty, as I should be of my wealth did I acquire it by servility and corruption."

"Sir," exclaimed the Judge, "you are forgetting the respect which you owe to the dignity of the judicial character."

"Dignity, my lord!" said the advocate. "When a person who is invested with the dignity of the judgement seat lays it aside for a moment to enter into a disgraceful personal contest, it is in vain when he has been worsted to seek to resume it, or to shelter himself behind an authority which he has voluntarily abandoned."

At this the Judge exploded, "Sir, if you say another word I shall commit you."

"In that event," was the quiet reply, "we both of us can reflect that I am not the worst thing your lordship has committed."

The bench crossed swords with Curran at its peril. FitzGibbon was once ill-advised enough to suggest that he was hair-splitting in attempting to distinguish between "also" and "likewise" which, he said, were obviously synonymous. He was informed: "I venture to disagree, my lord, the distinction is real. For many years the great Lord Lifford presided over this Court. You also preside over it, but not likewise."

There are two types of forensic insolence which were personified by Curran on the one hand and O'Connell on the other. Curran was the classic wit par excellence; his weapon was the verbal rapier which pierced to the vitals. It is doubtful if O'Connell can be classed as a wit at all, his weapons were stunning phrases with which he belaboured his opponents as with bludgeons, as when he called Disraeli "the lineal descendant of the impenitent thief'. He also reprimanded a court which had rejected evidence he had tendered, and which reconsidered its ruling the following day, by telling them: "If your lordships had known as much law yesterday as you do to-day, you would have avoided great inconvenience to the public, and distress to my client."

And yet again, he had the temerity to say to a judge: "I never took you for a model at the Bar, and your behaviour on the Bench has not been such as to give any reason to reconsider my original estimate of your character."

Each advocate has had his own lineal, or rather spiritual, descendants at the Irish Bar, and if such passages are now few, as the occasions for them are rare, from time to time they still take place.

It is not so very long ago since an emminent leader announced in the High Court that he appeared for the prosecutor in a prerogative matter, whereupon the presiding Judge inquired: "Who appears for the State?"

"I do," said counsel for the respondent.

"I'll hear the State," said the Judge.

"You will hear me," said the leader.

The astonished Judge drew a deep breath and observed icily: "Counsel will kindly remember that as long as I am presiding over this Court the procedure which I lay down will be observed."

"I can assure your lordship," was the retort, "that whenever I am appearing in this Court, I will ensure that the proper procedure is observed."

The shade of Curran must have approved!

A modern example of the O'Connell school was to be found in a case in the Circuit Court, the conduct of which was discreditable to both Judge and Counsel. The acrimonious exchanges ended when counsel threw his brief on the table and walked out of Court, but not before he had said: "As a member of the Bar of some standing, I refuse to be treated with levity, or be the target of the improper

156

observations of a temporary Judge who owes his elevation less to his legal merits than his political sychophancy."

It should be said, however, that interchanges between Bench and Bar, as indeed between lawyers generally, do not engender any lasting ill-will. It would be ludicrous were it otherwise as counsel are associated with each other, and solicitors, throughout their professional lives—on the same side to-day, opponents to-morrow, while it would be difficult for a judge to preside over a permanently antagonistic court.

It was not always so. As we are aware, duelling was a commonplace among the gentlemen of the long robe, and it may be said that the attorneys were, in this regard, very little less ready than the senior branch of the profession. The curious, to this day, may visit in a Sligo cemetery the grave of Robert W. Hillas, Counsellor-at-Law, who in 1814 was shot through the heart by a solicitor called Fenton in a duel over a dispute about fees. Incidentally, this case is also interesting as illustrating the view of society about this method of resolving an argument. Fenton was duly returned for trial before Mr. Justice Fletcher, and a Sligo jury. His lordship reviewed the facts, which were common case, and informed them that the law was plain, that it was a case of wilful murder, but that "By God, I never heard of a fairer duel in the whole course of my life." We are not surprised to learn that there was an acquittal.

Costs are a subject about which solicitors have always exhibited a marked and delicate sensitivity. In Fenton's day, we are told by Oliver Burke, the attorney would not hear of his client taxing his bill of costs. Such outrageous conduct was met with wholesome correction, and "as sure as an attempt of the kind was made, a horsewhipping and a duel followed."

If the relationship between counsel and the bench, and counsel and solicitor is, as a rule, uneventful and humdrum; as between counsel and client, particularly on the criminal side, it frequently creates situations and problems with which the text-books do not deal.

A barrister expects the confidence of his client. This trust, apart from any other consideration, will enable his case to be presented in the best light, and the pitfalls, as far as humanly possible, avoided. Every practitioner can tell rueful stories about the failure of rapport which has had disastrous results. One such failure was the lot of a certain young barrister at the very outset of his career.

Even his friends, of whom he had many, could not describe Charles as a matinée idol. He was rather less than under-sized, he had a broken and flattened nose, and when he walked he waddled like a duck. Shortly after his call, be-wigged and be-gowned, he was sitting in Green Street court, thinking the lonely thoughts of the briefless barrister. Suddenly, his fairy godmother, in the unlikely form of a solicitor's clerk, said to him, *sotto voce*: "I don't know your name, sir, but I would be very obliged if you could spare the time to do a little case of larceny, if you are free. I'm afraid the fee is only two guineas."

Oddly enough, Charlie had been reflecting that he had already been free for three months, and looked like being free for the rest of his life. However, having imparted his name, he graciously agreed to accept the brief and the fee. He was then led by his companion downstairs to the cells, one of which was duly opened by a warder on the impressive sight of learned counsel. The clerk entered briskly and Charlie toddled in after him.

The disconsolate prisoner was sitting on a bench looking at the floor and cogitating the injustice of the finger print system when the clerk slapped him on the shoulder and said: "Cheer up, Jem, I've got a barrister for you. This is the counsel who is going to defend you."

Jem looked at Charlie, gave a start of shock and cried: "Be the lord Harry, it's not bloody well fair! I'm going to appeal."

One of the many misconceptions the layman has about a barrister's life is that he is constantly the recipient of the humble thanks of grateful clients. Nothing could be further from the truth, and the barrister who does not obtain his fee in a criminal case before he goes to Court is due for a rude awakening. On this topic the advice of one of the best and most experienced defenders of prisoners at the Bar was, "Always get it when the tears are in his eyes."

If the breath of ingratitude is rude when, despite the best endeavours of his advisers, the client has been convicted, it is doubly so when he has been acquitted.

MacMahon, which was not his name, was charged in the Circuit Court "for that he did steal, take, and carry away two boxes of eels valued in or about £150, the property etc."

The circumstances were peculiar. Mr. MacMahon was well known—very well known—to the local police, who were in the habit almost every week-end of cooling him off in the station until he was sober enough to find his own way home. Apart from these runs-in with the law, he was never known to do anything else out of the way. Accordingly, when the boxes were stolen from the fisheries the breath of suspicion never brushed the heated brow of MacMahon.

One Saturday night, however, months after the larceny, the usual call came to the Civic Guard from a local public-house to collect him as he was becoming a little obstreperous. When the Guards were resignedly going through the usual ritual, MacMahon struggled free and addressed them as follows: "Take your dirty hands off me, yiz dumb peelers. Yiz'll never get me with the bloody eels now, because they're over beyant in London, and well eaten."

As a result of this ill-timed, but unquestionably voluntary, statement Mr. MacMahon found himself in the dock before a jury of his peers.

His learned counsel took the courageous, but only available, line of laughing the case out of Court. He had no difficulty in establishing in cross-examination that his client was drunk when he gave his unsolicited information to the police and, further, that there was absolutely no love whatever lost between the Guards and himself. Accordingly, when addressing the jury, he suggested that his client who, they could see, was little better than a simple-minded, harmless drunk, was merely indulging in what he probably thought was a brilliant display of humour, in mocking the police for their failure to catch the real culprit. He also suggested that the jury might form the view that a man of his client's mental calibre would not have the intelligence to bring off so well planned a coup as the Great Unsolved Eelbox Robbery.

The jury apparently thought so, because they acquitted with commendable despatch.

The final scene was reminiscent of the treatment Charles Phillips received at the hands of the Widow Wilkins. The victorious barrister was in the robing room, modestly acknowledging the congratulations of his brethren and the instructing solicitor, when the door burst open with a crash. It was his infuriated client who had arrived to add his personal tribute, which was a stunning right-hander under the jaw which prostrated his astonished advocate.

"That'll teach you to make a bloody laughing stock out of a decent man in front of the whole country, you blackguard!" he roared, and the door was slammed again.

At least the fee had been paid in advance.

Socially, there is not the same intimacy between counsel as in the days when travel was so much more difficult and barristers on Circuit lived together for long periods as members of a family. The circuit system still exists, and while the old camaraderie also exists, the motor car has greatly invaded the close association between the circuiteers who can now return each day to Dublin from towns where in former times they would live together for a week.

Neither is there the same social intercourse between the Judges and the Bar as there used to be, for similar reasons, except on the two occasions every year when the High Court sits in the country towns on Circuit. Even as recently as the years preceding the First World War things were very different, and in the last century so different that sometimes in their progress from town to town, which was a leisurely peregrination, the Judges and the Bar might not arrive until the afternoon, in which event his lordship would probably decide not to sit until after they all had dined. For that matter, some judges, even on an ordinary day, would adjourn the court in the afternoon, and resume at 8 p.m. after dinner. One of them used to justify these sittings on the ground that if Parliament could pass the laws at night, they could be administered at night. One gathers, however, that postprandial jurisprudence received a more liberal administration than is usual in the cold and sober light of day.

It is recounted that this particular nocturnal jurist ascended the bench at the Castlebar Assizes on the stroke of 8 o'clock one night, and after a few preliminary hiccups, announced his readiness to take up the next case. Thereupon, the Bar, who had also dined extremely well, bowed and took their places in the Court. A jury was sworn and a prisoner arraigned on a manslaughter charge to which he pleaded Not Guilty.

There was then a hiatus in the proceedings, during which counsel looked at each other to see who would open the ball. Eventually, the barrister who held the defence brief stood up and the following lunacy ensued: "May it please your lordship, gentlemen of the Jury, in this case it is my painful duty to appear for the prosecution."

At this the prisoner wailed: "Stop him! That's the man who was paid for defending me."

Counsel for the Prosecution: "That's a good one, you are for the defence; I suppose I must be for the prosecution."

Judge: "That is really an excellent joke—I mean to shay we must shift, I mean sift, every case that comes before us. Prisoner at the bar you have been convicted—"

Defence Counsel: "Your lordship anticipates, we have not tried him yet."

Judge: "These interruptions from the Bar are ill-timed and

unbecoming. It is impossible that I can sit here to be interrupted by counsel, and I must commit if there is a repetition of this sort of conduct. Prisoner at the bar, have you anything to say as to why I should not pass sentence on you."

Defence Counsel: "My learned friend has proved nothing against him, and I submit there is no case to go to the jury."

Judge: "Silence, sir! Gentlemen of the Jury, you have heard such of the facts of this distressing case as are capable of being conveyed to your knowledge. Gentlemen, the criminal law of this country draws a happy distinction between assumed guilt, and guilt actually proved. In Hawkins's *Pleas of the Crown* you will find all this laid down much better than I can explain it to you. I will therefore, not detain you with any further remarks but will now leave the case in your hands, with the simple observation that in the unlikely event of your having any doubt as to the guilt of the prisoner, you are bound to give him the benefit of that doubt."

The Jury to the Foreman: "Of course we must let him off, as we have heard nothing against him."

Foreman: "We find the prisoner, Not Guilty."

Judge: "Very well, it is your verdict, not mine. Prisoner at the Bar, you have had a very narrow escape. You may leave the dock, but I warn you that if you ever come before this Court again, you will certainly be transported."

This is, perhaps, an extreme instance of juristical conviviality, but it must be recorded in the interests of truth that the history of the Irish circuits is not one that would receive the imprimatur of the Friends of Temperance Society. Even up to quite recent times this regrettable tradition had been vigorously maintained, both by bench and bar. For instance, the famous Judge Day used to fill his inkwell with neat gin, and was wont to relieve the tedium of drawn out Chancery cases by imbibing it through a specially prepared quill pen.

A more modern devotee of Bacchus presided in the Midlands, and although the stories about him are legion, one in particular made an indelible impact on the annals of the Circuit.

A Rent Act application was the unlikely vehicle for this particular one of his lordship's more unconventional performances. It seems that the net point at issue was whether or not the premises, the subject matter of the application, were used mainly for residential or for business purposes. This issue was fiercely contested and a great body of evidence called on either side. His lordship confessed himself as being quite at a loss to determine where the truth lay. He also announced that as he represented the spirit and embodiment of the Law, his imperative concern was to see that justice was done, and that the only way out of the impasse lay in his visiting the premises himself, whatever personal inconvenience that course might entail. Accordingly, he adjourned the Court and the litigants, their solicitors, and counsel, and the Judge all set forth for the *locus in quo*, which was twelve miles away in the heart of the country.

This pronouncement took place on a Tuesday afternoon, just before the luncheon interval. It proved to be a very long interval indeed, for the learned gentlemen did not return that day. Wednesday came and went, and the court of Justice saw them not; nor did the errants return on Thursday morning. Late that afternoon, however, the Judge's crier, one Mr. Fisher, knocked at the door of the Barristers' room and interrupted a spirited game of poker by informing counsel that the Court was now reassembling. When they took their places they were not surprised to note that their brethren and their instructing solicitors were looking distinctly frail and somewhat shop-soiled.

His lordship, on the contrary, when he came out on the bench was in the best of humour, and was wearing a countenance glowing with bonhomie, and a wig precariously tilted on the side of his head. He then proceeded to deliver judgement: "I am happy, gentlemen, to be in a position now to say that the doubts which I had entertained in this extremely difficult and important case have been resolved. I have personally visited the premises, which are the subject matter of this dispute, and have been accompanied by learned counsel and their solicitors, for whose co-operation I take this opportunity of expressing my gratitude. As a result of my visit and my observation *in situ* of these premises, I have no hesitation whatever in deciding that they are mainly, indeed I may say solely, used for the purpose of the sale of alcoholic drink."

It was on this circuit that a venerable and erudite Chancery counsel mainly practised. He was beloved of his colleagues who every night were in the habit of assisting him to his room and seeing him safely to bed. One night he informed them that he had to get the night express to Dublin, so they drove him to the railway station and decanted him into his carriage, fast asleep. They were about to leave when the carriage door opened and a hand appeared holding a pair of boots, which were carefully deposited on the platform!

There was another counsel who practised on the Southern Circuit who was equally famous, and an authentic story is told about him which was later attributed to W. C. Fields, the comedian. For the benefit of the solicitors, this character announced at the outset of one Circuit that he was going "on the dry" for life. In pursuance of this pledge, whenever the rounds of drinks were coming up to the bar mess at night, he always asked for a glass of ginger ale. To the knowledge of his brethren he had made a surreptitious arrangement with the waiter to add a large Scotch to this beverage. No one exposed this pleasant fiction until he did so himself. One night he was called out to the telephone, and one of the junior circuiteers took the opportunity of substituting a glass of unfortified ginger ale for the drink which had just been served. His senior shortly returned and immediately took a deep draught out of his glass. He incontinently spat it out and roared: "If I get the blackguard that has put ginger ale into my ginger ale, I'll murder him."

The other end of the country also witnessed doughty deeds. Not so many years ago it was the custom in Derry for the Lord Mayor and Burgesses to welcome the Judges of the Assize to the city in a ceremony on the steps of the Guild Hall. Their lordships were attended by the members of the bar and all sorts of legal dignitaries, and were driven in a coach preceded by a troop of mounted cavalry. There were invariably thousands of spectators on the route and crowding the historic walls. One day the impressive procession was completed by a bread-van, on the driving seat of which were perched two eminent members of the Junior Bar in their wigs and gowns, while the legitimate driver, who had been suitably entertained, slumbered peacefully in the back among the loaves. The Lord Mayor was doubly gratified to observe that one of the learned gentlemen was his own son.

It may also be noted that solicitors could point to members who could bear comparison in festive prowess with the other branch of the profession. Indeed, in that regard they were even more favourably placed in that the members of the magistrates bench, before which they usually appeared, were not conspicuously abstemious themselves. The sort of thing they did in court with impunity was hair-raising. On one occasion, Mackey, the Crown Solicitor for County Donegal, was opposing a solicitor called Boyle. Boyle, who was a first-class performer and as shrewd as a fox, was a small man of about five feet nothing in his shoes. He was universally known as But Boyle, because of his propensity for prefacing his every observation with that conjunction. Both himself and Mackey had been entertaining each other in a nearby tavern before going into court and the proceedings were, consequently, even more lively than usual, all of Mackey's antithetical periods being punctuated by a machine gun fire of "buts" from his diminutive opponent. At last Mackey, who was a very tall, well-built man, could stand it no longer and he turned on him and said, "One more interruption from you Mr. Boyle and I'll pick you up and put you in my pocket," which evoked the reply, "If you did that, Mackey, you'd have a damn sight more brains in your bottom than you have in your head."

If the world "fabulous" had not been appropriated by teenagers to describe the moronic providers of their entertainment, it could properly be applied to Mackey. One of his best exploits was when he had come to the end of a particularly hectic week in London and was suffering from that Stygian gloom which is the wages of revelry. He was also suffering from that ineffable yearning for his native heath, to which the exiled Irishman is incurably prone. It descended upon him when he was standing aimlessly in Piccadilly Circus and was so exigent that he hailed and entered a passing taxi.

"Where to, sir?" said the driver.

"Ramelton, please," said Mackey.

"Beg your pardon sir," from the driver.

"Ramelton, County Donegal, man," barked Mr. Mackey.

The driver never batted an eye. He drove Mackey on to the night-boat from Liverpool and off again at Belfast, and thence to his home in Ramelton in the very north of Donegal.

Not every trespass on the indulgence of the Court was committed by advocates who had looked on the wine when it was red. Every profession has its characters to whom a licence is given by authority, which would be unthinkable for the ordinary practitioner. In this connexion at the Irish Bar the name of John Devlin immediately springs to mind. John carefully fostered the impression that he was a harmless and rather naïve innocent, a rock upon which many an unwary opponent perished. It is difficult to convey the sheer beauty of some of his performances as no printer's ink can reproduce a Dublin accent on which you could hang your hat.

One which the Bar still joyously remembers was an appeal from a decision of Judge Shannon in his favour, which came before Mr. Justice Gavan Duffy, President of the High Court. The appellant's counsel was a rather pompous ass and he opened the case in his most portentous manner by saying: "Ordinarily, my lord, I would be hesitant to criticize a de-

cision of that careful and learned lawyer, Judge Shannon. I
can only characterize the judicial aberration which gives rise
to this appeal as a case of Homer nodding."

At the end of the case the President began his judgement
by saying: "I am satisfied that the learned Circuit Court
Judge was correct, and I dismiss the appeal."

Whereupon John Devlin interjected a stage whisper that
could be heard on the other side of the Liffey: "Homer nods
again!"

One of the kindest of men, but as so often happens one of
the most irascible, was the late Mr. Justice Hanna. On the
bench he was quick-witted and impatient, and woe betide the
errant counsel who was not present when his case came on
for second calling as it would be irrevocably struck out. One
day, John Devlin found himself in the unenviable position
of having a motion in Hanna's Probate list and also a case in
the Police Court. It should be said that the High Court is
extremely jealous of its dignity, and while Counsel will be
forgiven if he has been engaged in the Supreme Court or
another of the High Courts, he will get short shrift if his non-
appearance is because of his activities in an inferior tribunal.
Despite this, John decided to take a chance, did his police
court case with unseemly haste, and rushed into the Probate
Court: "May it please your lordship."

"Yes, Mr. Devlin."

"May I mention the motion of In the Goods of Amelia
Mulligan, deceased, my lord?"

"You most certainly may not, Mr. Devlin," said Mr.
Justice Hanna, "that motion was called twice and has been
struck out."

"So I understand, my lord, but I would very respectfully
urge on you to reinstate it."

"On what grounds, Mr. Devlin?"

"My lord, I was unavoidably detained in another court."

"And may I inquire what court, Mr. Devlin?'

"Ah, my lord," pleaded John, "please don't ask me that,
it would only make it worse."

It is hardly necessary to add that the case was reinstated. Any other counsel would probably have been sentenced to death!

One other anecdote about the inimitable John is irresistible. No man had a better knowledge of the rules of evidence when it suited him; when it did not, he maltreated them in a manner that must have made the late Messrs. Phipson and Best turn somersaults in their respective graves. One such occasion arose in another case before Judge Shannon. Mr. Devlin was examining his client, the defendant, in a running-down case:

"I suppose, sir, you were driving hard in on your left hand side of the road at the time?"

"Really," protested the agonized opponent, "surely there is a limit to the latitude which even Mr. Devlin is allowed in examination of his own witness!"

"Oh, very well," said the imperturbable John, "if my friend is so punctilious." He turned again to his witness and said: "Now, sir, I don't want to lead you, so will you tell my lord and the jury were you this distance, or this, from the left hand kerb when the collision took place?"

This appalling question was illustrated by learned counsel first holding his two hands about six inches apart, and then about twelve.

His opponent gave it up!

Reverting to the judiciary there can be no question but that to-day it functions in a pleasanter atmosphere in every court, from the Supreme Court downwards, than ever before. Religious or political bitterness no longer envenoms its conduct or its decisions, as so often happened in former, and not so remote, times.

Prior to the passing of the Catholic Emancipation Act in 1829, no Catholic, which meant the vast majority of the Irish, could be admitted to the Bench, the Inner Bar or even the Magistracy. The people now thought that the leaven of native blood in the judiciary would act as a corrective. The event was to prove them sadly mistaken, as a minority of the farseeing had foretold. In return for preferment, the new men proved themselves even more willing instruments of Government policy than the old. There now grew up an anomalous class, despised by both the Ascendancy to which it aspired and the people from whom it sprang. Thackeray first immortalized it in his *Irish Sketch Book*, while in Ireland its members were known, with amused contempt, as "Cawstle Cawtholics", and Dublin, where they principally flourished, as "The City of Dreadful Knights."

The career of Mr. Justice Keogh, of the Court of Common Pleas, if an extreme example of perfidy, is instructive. He was born in Lower Gardiner Street, Dublin, and was called to the Bar in 1840 at the age of twenty three. Possessed of that type of meretricious charm, which is the charlatan's stock-in-trade, he ingratiated himself with his brethren and solicitors and quickly obtained a good practice in which, admittedly, he displayed ability. In 1846, when in London, during the Long Vacation he was introduced to a prominent and extremely rich Jewish financier. In those days anti-Semitism was rife in London society, and Keogh, who had ever an eye to the main chance, by flattery, hypocrisy and deference so insinuated himself into his good graces that the gratified tycoon placed his bank balance at the young barrister's disposal, and backed him as candidate for the borough of Athlone in the 1847 election. With this support and that of the Catholic clergy, whom he had also assiduously courted, he was returned.

This was the last year of the Great Famine and now came the aftermath. Eighteen forty-eight was the year of revolution all over Europe, and Ireland had her own tragi-comic Young Ireland uprising. The social conditions were appalling. There was wholesale bankruptcy among the landlords, and tenants, who were unable even to buy food far less pay their rack-rents, were evicted by the thousand. Thus, in 1850 came into existence the Tenants' Right League with the object of obtaining the three Fs: Fair Rents, Fixity of Tenure and

Freedom of Sale. Closely allied with this movement, for no particularly logical reason, was the Catholic Defence Association. This was a clerically inspired organization which was less concerned with the wrongs of the people than the status of the hierarchy, which was being depreciated by Lord John Russell's Ecclesiastical Titles Bill. The leading lay lights of this Association were Keogh and John Sadleir, a shady Tipperary banker.

Again Keogh went forward for Athlone and on June 26 1852 a meeting was held there in favour of Civil and Religious Liberty, and of Tenant Right. It was on this platform that Keogh made his famous "So help me God" speech, which he was never to live down. In the course of it he swore in the most solemn way that he would never rest, nor give support to any Government, until the great objects of liberty and tenant right had been achieved. Throughout the campaign so many different variations were played by Sadleir and Keogh on this theme, and that of protestation of zeal and loyalty for the old Faith, that they were known as "The Pope's Brass Band".

The hopes of a desperate people had been raised to the skies by the results of the elections. The parties were so nearly equal in strength that the Irish party held the balance of power and could dictate their terms. Nothing, therefore, can describe the shock which stunned the country when Lord Aberdeen announced the new ministerial appointments, for they included the names of John Sadleir as a Junior Lord of the Treasury, and the Right Hon. William Keogh as Solicitor General for Ireland. With the renegades, there also defected nineteen of their Catholic Defence mercenaries, all of whom were suitably rewarded. The cause of agrarian justice was set back half a century. The Hierarchy defended Sadleir and Keogh on the grounds that they had been promised that the Ecclesiastical Titles Act would be allowed to fall into disuse; it was a championship they were to live to rue.

Mr. Keogh's progress to the Bench was swift. In six weeks

the Aberdeen Government gave way to that of Palmerston, thereby giving the Solicitor General another opportunity to effect a double-cross. He had agreed with Brewster, the Attorney General, that both would decline to accept office under the new administration. Brewster duly resigned and having done so, informed Keogh who immediately obtained his friend's job. That was on February 10 1855. The very following year the death of Judge Torrens created a vacancy in the Common Pleas to which, by tradition, the Attorney General was entitled to be appointed.

Thus, at the age of thirty-nine, the recreant who had betrayed his people, his trust and his friends, and was soon to apostatize from his religion, was elevated to the Bench as the Right Honourable Mr. Justice Keogh, one of Her Majesty's Judges of the Common Pleas. At least in his incumbency of his judicial office his conduct was consistent, and for the next twenty years on the bench he never deviated for an instant from the narrow path of infamy on which he had set his course.

His lordship was also a financial crook. His close association with John Sadleir continued until the failure of the Tipperary Bank in the biggest crash in Irish commercial history when Sadleir poisoned himself at midnight on Hampstead Heath to avoid arrest. Thousands of small investors and depositors lost every penny of their life savings, and the most piteous scenes took place as they stood dumbly outside the closed doors of the Bank waiting for them to open so that they could draw their money. Two ex-members of the "Brass Band" managed to escape to the Continent, but the scandal of implicating a High Court Judge was too much for the Government to stomach and Mr. Justice Keogh was not even charged.

The two highlights of his career on the Bench were first, when he was one of the presiding Judges appointed to the Special Commission in November 1865 to try the leaders of the Fenians. The principal of these were O'Leary, Luby and O'Donovan Rossa, the first two of whom were sentenced to

twenty years penal servitude, and Rossa to the term of his
natural life. This savagery shocked even the most extreme
and the sentences were later commuted.

In Rossa's trial Keogh proved himself a worthy successor
of his distinguished predecessor in the Common Pleas, Lord
Norbury. The Attorney General had put in evidence against
him various copies of the newspaper *The Irish People*, which
he edited. Rossa, who defended himself, immediately insisted on his right to read the whole file, but he said he would
not detain their lordships by reading the advertisements. The
Bench could not dispute his right to adopt this course, as the
Attorney General's conduct of the case had made all the
newspapers evidence. Rossa then began with Vol. 1 Issue 1,
and particularly emphasized the articles, most of which he
had written himself, which dealt with the career of Mr. Justice Keogh. These literary efforts showed that considerable
research had preceded their composition, but it cannot be
said that his lordship showed his appreciation. In fact, as one
might expect, he behaved abominably.

In any criminal trial it is the tradition, within reason, to
give every indulgence to the defence. Where the accused
appears in person this latitude is even more generously extended. Keogh, on the contrary, refused to adjourn at all for
luncheon, and had his meal sent in to the bench. The same
thing happened at dinner time and Rossa, debilitated as he
was from months in a prison cell, fell back in the dock exhausted. All during his ordeal he had been mocked, interrupted and bullied by the Judge, who now took pleasure in
delivering a hypocritical homily, and sentenced him to be
"kept in penal servitude for the term of his natural life."

There was another disgraceful element in this trial. By
reason of the nature of the evidence, consisting largely as it
did of an attack on the presiding judge, he should have dis-
qualified himself. In later days a new trial would certainly
have been ordered by the Court of Criminal Appeal on the
ground that not merely must Justice be done, but it must be
seen to be done.

The trials of O'Leary and Luby were almost as discreditable, and the best comment on Keogh's behaviour was composed by Doctor, later Judge, Webb, who was certainly no friend of Fenianism:

> Capricious Goddess who by pitch and toss
> Doth still award the diadem and cross
> What different fates await the Fenians here
> The fools that are so and the rogues that were
> The felon's dock awaits O'Leary so
> The seat of judgement is the seat of Keogh;
> Thrice happy Keogh who if he's not belied
> Now tries the crimes for which he was not tried
> And seated on the bench doth safely mock
> The nobler felon standing in the dock.

The second highlight of the Judge's career was the great Galway Election Petition in 1872 in which he was appointed Commissioner to inquire into the election of Captain John Philip Nolan, the Nationalist candidate who, by 2,823 votes to 658 defeated Captain William le Poer Trench. This inquiry was held in Galway Courthouse and lasted for two months. In support of the petition Captain Trench, Lord Westmeath, Lord Delvin, Sir Thomas Burke, Lord Gough and a miscellany of land-agents and bailiffs were examined. Against it appeared Archbishop McHale of Tuam, Bishops McEvilly and Duggan of Galway and Clonfert, a large number of priests and, of course, the candidate and his agent.

In his judgement, which lasted eight hours, the cidevant leader of the Pope's Brass Band scarified the three bishops, and named thirty-two priests whom he held guilty of improper electoral practices. He unseated Nolan, who was condemned in costs to the tune of £14,000. His lordship's language was of a tone and violence more appropriate to the tavern than the forum of justice. No judicial performance in the last century produced such a sensation, but it was his swan-song. Every treachery and perfidy, every piece of knavery and infidelity in his career, and they were many, were now resurrected and he was attacked as never was a judge attacked before. It unhinged his mind.

He lingered on for a few years suffering from advanced melancholia. In September 1878 he attempted to kill his attendant, and commit suicide, and on September 30 he died at Bingen in Germany.

Keogh was, of course, unique, but it is not unfair to say that practically every appointment to the superior courts up to the Treaty were of men who basked in the radiance that shone from Dublin Castle. Johnny Moriarity, who ended as Lord Justice of Appeal, had a political career that would make the Vicar of Bray seem, by comparison, like an ever-fixed mark. He was successively Liberal, Tory, and Liberal, until at last he got aboard the Nationalist barque which steered him safely into the fair haven of the Court of Appeal. The reason for Mr. Moriarity's unremitting search for the ultimate political truth was that judicial, and indeed all legal, appointments were dispensed only to those deserving of the bounty of the Government in power.

It is also fair to say that while few were capable of the *tours-de-force* of the volatile Moriarity there were those who turned some pretty agile somersaults when the Government changed. Whatever their political affiliations, however, once they had achieved the rank of Judge, or Law Officer, they never forgot that the fountain of honour was also the fountain of honours, and was situated far away from any Irish river, on the banks of the Thames. Of such an order was Peter O'Brien who, as Attorney General, brought the art of jury-packing to a perfection that even Saurin had never contemplated, in somewhat the same way as Berry the hangman improved upon the technique of his predecessor, Marwood. O'Brien was in due course rewarded with the Lord Chief Justiceship of Ireland under the resounding style and title of Lord O'Brien of Kilfenora; he is better known to legal history, however, as "Pether the Packer."

The attitude of these dependants on the Imperial patronage is clearly spelled out by A. M. Sullivan in his book *The Last of the Sergeants*. Sullivan was one of those Irish patriots whom the Four Courts bred like a culture of bacilli, and was for ever protesting his fierce and undying love of country. These Roman sentiments he was careful never to allow to interfere with his own personal advancement and, accordingly, he regarded the Insurrection of 1916, and the Treaty of 1921 as unmitigated disasters. He greeted the foundation of the Irish State with an epitaph and a prophecy: "The dream of Ireland a Nation has persisted in the Celtic mind for two thousand years, and, in spite of recent disaster, there will be people to go on dreaming of it for a thousand years more."

In the same book he differs from William Butler Yeats who referred to the Rising as the birth of "A Terrible Beauty" by dismissing it as a "murderous riot".

The beginning of the valedictory passage in which Sullivan bids farewell to the country for which he had always avowed devotion, while it is hardly calculated to tug at the heartstrings, is worth reproducing:

"You cannot transplant an oak at fifty." Grattan's warning kept running through my mind as I sat in the judges' chambers, checking and signing the orders "by the Lords Justice of Assize" at the close of the last assizes held in the old Kingdom of Ireland. I had delivered the last charge to the Grand Jury. Lloyd George had agreed to hand over twenty-six counties to the anti-British, and six counties to the anti-Irish. I suddenly realised that I had made up my mind to leave the country and I had to make the choice of going east or west. My choice, in fact, had been predetermined...."

The strains of *Come Back to Erin* did not reach him from across the Irish Sea, as his countrymen recognized that Sullivan, whom they described as the last of the recruiting Sergeants, represented to a degree that type of rootless Irish lawyer which was not the least defect of the Irish administration. If only for that reason, the ruminations of the departing Sergeant are illuminating.

It should be said that this deference to the policy of the executive was displayed only in trials, generally on the criminal side, involving political considerations. In its day-to-day discharge of its duties the standard of the Irish Judiciary was extremely high and, in particular, the decisions of the Irish

Chancery Courts were always accorded the greatest respect across the water. The story was the same at the Irish Bar where the level of advocacy was infinitely higher than in any other part of the then United Kingdom. The meteoric success in London, for example, of Edward Carson, was always a source of wonder to his brethren in Dublin where his ability, although respected, was not considered outstanding.

It would not be correct to say that the signing of the Treaty represented for the legal system a complete break with the past. There is a continuity in the Common Law which was unaffected by the new dispensation. The Statute Law was also taken over intact except for such enactments or portions of enactments, as were repugnant to the provisions of the Constitution. For instance, to name only one, it would be scarcely logical to attract The Restoration of Order (Ireland) Act into the corpus of a system, the institution of which that Act had been designed to abort. The really radical innovation was in the provision, in place of the unwritten British Constitution, of the written Constitution of 1922. This, thenceforward, was to be the fundamental law of the land, and any other law declared to be inconsistent with it would be invalid to the extent of its repugnancy.

The Courts set up by the young State differed in description, although not greatly in function, from those which they replaced. At the apex of the pyramid is the Supreme Court, then comes the High Court, one of the branches of which is the Central Criminal Court with jurisdiction over every type of crime. Next is the Circuit Court, which ranks somewhat higher than the old County Court, and lower than the High Court. All the judges of these courts are robed and wear the short judge's wig. The judge is addressed as My Lord and is referred to as His Lordship. Counsel appear before them in wigs and gowns and, while it is not necessary for them to be robed for their appearances in the District Court, it is not uncommon to be so attired as a matter of courtesy. Finally, as we have seen, the old magistrates bench was once and for all abolished.

The system may be said to have got properly under way with the setting up of the Circuit Courts and the abolition of the old County Courts in 1927, and on the whole it has worked successfully, for which the personnel of its first appointments may largely be thanked. The members of the first Supreme Court, Chief Justice Kennedy, and Fitzgibbon and Murnaghan J. J., were really first class judges, and the High Court formed an incomparably stronger bench than its immediate predecessors, and to that extent there was a change, pronouncedly for the better.

By and large also, as far as Bench and Bar are concerned, it is true to say *plus ça change, plus c'est la même chose*, and their joint association throughout the country still produces its legal folklore, as in former times.

There was, for instance, the seduction case which came for hearing before the learned Circuit Court Judge sitting at Ballyshannon, in the County of Donegal—not, be it said, his present lordship. It appears that the parties to this unfortunate action hailed from the village of Laghy, a hamlet which claims the distinction of being the stronghold of the most puritannical sect in Ulster. Despite these rigid tenets this was not the first case of its kind that had its genesis in the area. It was, however, unusual for such disputes to come to the notice of the Courts, as the time honoured procedure had hitherto been to hold a meeting of the elders of the community who would, if satisfied of the merits, award a sum as solatium to the injured lady.

This was a plain case and his lordship had no trouble in finding the facts proved and awarding as damages the sum of £75 and costs. At this the very young barrister who was representing the defendant was ill-advised enough to stand up and inform the Judge: "With respect, My Lord, I do not think Your Lordship has adverted to the fact that this a Laghy case."

"I am afraid I do not understand you," said the Judge.

"My solicitor instructs me", said the neophyte, "that never

has there been an award of more than £25 in a Laghy case of this nature."

"I am grateful for that information," replied His Lordship politely, "which, however, is now of merely historical legal interest, for you may tell your solicitor to advise his clients that, as from today, the rate for seduction in Laghy has appreciated by two hundred per cent."

Perhaps it would be appropriate to take leave of the modern Bench with a cautionary tale, involving all three Courts, the High, the Circuit and the District, which could well be gothically entitled The Judge's Revenge.

The late Circuit Court Judge Gleeson never disguised his scorn for the decisions of the Court of Criminal Appeal, which he always pointedly referred to as the Criminal Court of Appeal. This disdain was not unconnected with the circumstance that many of his own charges to juries had received some pretty rough treatment at the hands of that august tribunal. In this regard, perhaps the worst offender from his point of view was the late Mr. Justice Hanna, who was also probably the best criminal lawyer in the superior courts.

It appears that one year, Judge Hanna during the Long Vacation found himself at a loose end in a Midland town which was on Judge Gleeson's circuit. For want of anything better to do he strolled into the back of the local District Court which was sitting. He was at once spotted by the District Justice who insisted that he come up on the bench, and sit beside him. It so happened that a particularly abstruse point of law arose in the case at hearing which was argued at great length by the contending solicitors. His lordship became extremely interested, and when at the end of the case the Justice asked him, in a whisper, what the legal position was, Hanna suggested that he reserve his judgement for a fortnight and that he would let him have his opinion after he looked up the authorities in Dublin.

His Worship was delighted, and was doubly so when in about a week's time he received a long and closely reasoned opinion referred to all the authorities on the point, and running into about twenty pages of the High Court Judge's handwriting. This learned opinion the D.J. then proceeded to deliver as his own judgement, and to his gratification it received considerable publicity in the local press. But the end was not yet. To his astonishment, the defeated litigant appealed the decision to the Circuit Court sitting at Longford.

The Judge, it is hardly necessary to say, knew perfectly well what had happened and whose judgement was under appeal, but not even the most oblique reference had been made to the fact that the District Justice had merely acted as a mouthpiece for the Honourable Mr. Justice Hanna. He also knew that everyone in Court was aware of the position; all of which filled his judicial heart with a pure and malicious glee.

His judgement was a masterpiece. There could be no appeal from his decision in a District Court appeal, and so he was at large. He parsed, analysed and tore to shreds every proposition in the judgement that had been delivered, and finished up by saying: "It is, therefore, my duty to reverse the decision of the learned District Justice, which I do with all the more reluctance as he has obviously given a considerable amount of time and trouble to his judgement. I defer to nobody in my admiration for his legal attainments, but I appreciate that remote as it is from legal sources it is often difficult for the District Court to apply authorities with precision. I can only assume in this case that the Justice was misled by the persuasiveness of the solicitor for the Plaintiff in reading the general principles as expressed in the text-books, as I find that where decided cases are referred to, they are either irrelevant to the point at issue, or are authorities for propositions contrary to those to which the learned Justice suggests that they are favourable. Accordingly, I have no difficulty in allowing this appeal, with costs in both Courts."

Never was a sweeter revenge, and never a finer example of a jurisprudence free from all restraint and awe.

# 10

## *The Sceptred Isle*

The adherence of the Irish to the monarchical principle goes back to the remotest times of prehistory. Every Irish child has been nurtured on the stirring legends of the invading Firbolgs and the fairy race of the Tuatha Dedannans, who contended for the throne long before the advent of Saint Patrick; and on Knocknarea, the Royal Hill, near Sligo, may be seen the burial mound of the beautiful and bloodthirsty Queen Maeve, who so notably demonstrated that the female of the species is more deadly than the male.

Right up to the day when Roderick submitted to the overlordship of the Norman, Henry II, Ireland always had her High King. If most of these monarchs met violent ends, there was always a mettlesome spirit ready to assume the sovereignty, just as certain South American Republics never lack aspirants to their precarious presidencies. It is also significant that the greatest hero in recorded and authentic Irish history is King Brian Boru; so much so that there are very few Irishmen who are not proud to trace their descent to him.

Nearly seven hundred years later we find devotion to the royal cause burning as fiercely as ever, and at the Battle of the

Boyne thousands of Irishmen on either side cheerfully mas-
sacred each other for the privilege of determining the respective claims of King Billy or King James to sit on the Throne
of Ireland.

The penal laws which followed this conflict did nothing to
cool the royal ardour of the native Irish, and a long memorial
from the insurgents at the time of the '98 Rebellion, while
setting out the melancholy catalogue of their grievances, was
at pains to protest undying loyalty and allegiance to the person of His Gracious Majesty, King George III.

Nor was the Great Liberator, Daniel O'Connell, ever anything but a royalist, as he proved by his fervent protestations
of loyalty to the day he died. His actions, indeed, spoke even
louder and more spectacularly when he joined the Yeomanry
in the year of the Emmett Rising, or rushed enthusiastically
into the sea to welcome to his native shore that attractive
monarch, George IV.

And so it went on. It is worthy of notice that the worst
malediction that an Irishman can pronounce is "The Curse
of Cromwell on you", thereby calling on the dark power of
the wicked regicide. As against that, he invests his own
leaders with the aura of majesty, so that Parnell was the
"Uncrowned King", and the most popular refrain
during the Trouble was "We'll crown De Valera King of
Ireland."

In view of this historical background with its tradition of
royal allegiance, it is not surprising that, alone of the
Dominions, Ireland, at the time of the so-called Abdication
Crisis, refused to obey the call to send her Prime Minister to
London to assist in the unthroning of His Majesty, King
Edward VIII. Instead, as is explained in the appendix to this
chapter, in her own domestic Parliament and by virtue of
ingenious and carefully contrived measures, she ensured that
King Edward would continue to rule over that part of the
country which was bound to him by the most solemn ties. At
that time, it was known as the Irish Free State. Since then, it

has been described, inaccurately and unconstitutionally, as the Republic of Ireland.

In these enlightened days, however, the time for rancour is past, and perhaps a happy compromise between the Monarchists and the Republicans can be effected by re-naming the country The Royal Irish Republic.

# Appendix

The title King of Ireland was first conferred on Henry VIII and his heirs and successors, Kings of England, by the enactment 33 Hen. VIII, Cap. 1 1542. The succession to the throne was, after the Glorious Revolution, established by the Bill of Rights, 1688 (1 Wm. & Mary, Sess. 2. Cap. 2). William and Mary were thereby declared King and Queen jointly of "England, France, and Ireland, and the dominions thereunto belonging."

The Act of Settlement, 12 and 13 Wm. III Cap. 2 (1700) made further provision for the succession in default of issue of William (Mary had died childless) and of Her Highness Princess Anne of Denmark, next in line, whose only son, Prince William, Duke of Gloucester, had also died. This Act settled the further succession on Princess Sophia, Electress of Hanover (grand-daughter of James I), and her issue.

The Act, 6 Anne, Cap. II (1706)—the Union of England and Scotland—provided for the continuance of the succession as already established; and the Act of Union of Great Britain and Ireland 1800) made similar provision.

The Treaty between Great Britain and Ireland of 1921 by Article I gave the latter country,* henceforward to be known as the Irish Free State, the same constitutional status in the Community of Nations known as the British Empire as the Dominion of Canada and the other Dominions with a Par-

* It should be noted that the jurisdiction of the Irish Free State Parliament did not extend to the six counties comprising Northern Ireland. See Treaty Articles 11 and 12.

liament having powers to make laws for the peace, order and good government of Ireland.

The position of the Irish Free State in relation to the Imperial Parliament was the same as that of Canada and the law, practice and constitutional usage governing the relation of the Crown to the Dominion of Canada was to govern its relationship to the Irish Free State. This is most important, and makes perfectly clear that the Irish Free State had no power whatsoever to alter the succession to the throne; a proposition which is accepted by constitutional lawyers. It is likewise axiomatic that the Dominion Parliaments had at that time no power to make laws having extra-territorial effect.

The Irish Free State Constitution of 1922, which was itself made subject to the Treaty, by Article 73 provided that, subject to the Constitution, the laws then in force in the Irish Free State were to continue until repealed or amended by the Oireachtas, which term means the law-making authority of the State, corresponding to the King in Parliament in the United Kingdom.

At this point, it should be emphasized that the laws touching the succession were constitutional laws of the Imperial Parliament, fundamental to the unity of the Empire and imposing a common allegiance on all subjects of the Crown, and could not be said, therefore, to be laws of the nature contemplated by Article 73. They were constitutional Acts governing the Irish Free State, antecedent and superior to its laws.

The Statute of Westminster, 1931, recites the results of the Imperial Conferences of 1926, 1929 and 1930. The Crown is "the symbol of the free association of the members of the British Commonwealth of Nations, and as they are united by a common allegiance to the Crown, it would be in accord with the established constitutional position of all the members . . . that any alteration in the *law* touching the succession . . . shall hereafter require the assent of all . . . ". It is further recited "that no law hereafter made by the Parlia-

184

ment of the United Kingdom shall extend to any of the Dominions otherwise than at the request and with the assent of that Dominion."

This clearly establishes that the law of succession was an Imperial Law which the United Kingdom Parliament would thereafter alter only with the assent of the Dominions.

It now becomes necessary to consider the acts in the law and events of December 1936.

On December 10 1936 Edward VIII signed what is called an Instrument of Abdication, but was in fact *nothing of the kind*—it is merely a declaration of his determination to renounce and his *desire* that effect be given to it.

On December 11 1936 the United Kingdom Parliament passed His Majesty's Declaration of Abdication Act 1936 (Cap. 3) with the assent (recited) of Canada, Australia, New Zealand and South Africa (but not that of the Irish Free State). This Act expressly provided for the demise of the Crown and for the succession to the Throne, *but it did not* extend to, and had therefore no effect in, the Irish Free State (cf. Statute of Westminster 1931). On the same day the Oireachtas passed the Constitution Amendment, No. 27 Act of 1936, deleting references to the King and his representative from the Constitution. This Act merely purported to deprive him of his Irish domestic functions. It did not, as it could not, deprive him of his title or prerogatives.

On the following day, December 12, was passed the Executive Authority (External Relations) Act 1936. This Act had been introduced in the Dail on the 11th, but was debated and signed on December 12 by the Chairman of the Dail who, by virtue of the Constitution Amendment Act No. 27, was authorized to do so in place of the Governor General, whose functions as the King's representative were also deleted from the Constitution.

The Executive Authority Act purported to provide that for certain purposes the King recognized by the other Dominions was authorized to act. These purposes (appointment of diplomatic and consular representatives and the conclusion of international agreements) would have been discharged by the Governor General up to the abolition of that office on the previous day.

It also provided that the Instrument of Abdication (recited) "shall have effect according to the tenor thereof." In so declaring, the Oireachtas was acting *ultra vires*, and furthermore if it were to be contended that it was not the provision would in any event be a nullity.

It was *ultra vires* because, as has been seen, it was not within the competence of the Oireachtas to alter the succession to the Throne. It would be a nullity because effect could not be given to the Instrument "*according to the tenor*" for two compelling reasons:

(a) The Instrument was not an abdication, but merely a Declaration of an intention to be carried out in the future. Incidentally, the British Act did not fall into this error, but went on expressly to enact that "there shall be a demise of the Crown."

(b) The Instrument recited Edward as being King of Great Britain, Ireland, etc. etc. but by virtue of the British Act he had already ceased to be King of Great Britain and the other Dominions, in fact, as of the last moment of December 10. Since that Act did not extend to the Irish Free State he was, beyond argument, *King of the Irish Free State* on December 11, and the Act did not purport to deal with the abdication from *that* Crown.

The important portion of the Executive Authority Act to which the above observations relate is at Section 3. Subsection (1) of that section provides that "so long as the Irish Free State is in association with Australia, Canada, Great Britain, New Zealand, and South Africa, and so long as the king recognised by these nations as the symbol of their co-operation, continues to act on behalf of each of those nations (on the advice of the respective governments thereof) for the purposes of the appointment of diplomatic and consular representatives, and the conclusion of international agreements, the king so *recognised* may, and is hereby authorised to, act on behalf of the Irish Free State for the *like* purposes, as and when advised by the Executive Council so to do."

Sub-section (2) goes on to enact that "immediately upon the passing of this Act (December 12 1936) the instrument of abdication executed by His Majesty King Edward VIII on December 10 1936 (a copy whereof is set out in this Act) shall have effect according to the tenor thereof and His said Majesty shall for the purposes of the foregoing subsection of this section, and all other (if any) purposes, cease to be king, and the king *for those purposes* [author's italics] shall henceforth be the person who if His said Majesty had died on the 10th of December 1936 unmarried, would for the time being be his successor under the law of the Irish Free State."

It should again be emphasized in this last connexion that, as has already been seen, there was no law of the Irish Free State providing for the succession to the Throne. Further, if this provision were valid, it would relate only to the exercise of executive functions (which is the only meaning that can be attached to "purposes"), as it must be construed as *ejusdem generis* with "purposes" in subsection (1); it most certainly cannot, even by the most elastic exercise of the rules of construction, be regarded as relating to the prerogatives of His Majesty.

Again, it is axiomatic that no law binds the Crown unless by express words, or necessary implication.

The Constitution of 1937 which was adopted by referendum on July 1 1937 and came into force on December 29 1937 did not itself effect any change in the constitutional position of the Crown, and it was announced by the British Government on December 29 1937, "They are prepared to treat the new Constitution as not effecting a fundamental alteration in the position of the Irish Free State, in future to be described . . . as Eire or Ireland, as a member of the British Commonwealth of Nations."

Article 29. 4. 2° of the Constitution provides that "for the purpose of the exercise of any executive function of the State in or in connection with its external relations the Government may . . . avail of or adopt any organ, instrument, or method of procedure used or adopted . . . by the members of any group or league of nations with which the state is or becomes associated for the purpose of international co-operation in matters of common interest."

This Article was clearly intended to give continued 'force to the Executive Authority (External Relations) Act, 1936, and the Government continued to make use of the then King of the United Kingdom and the other Dominions for certain purposes.

Article 12 of the Constitution of 1937 creates the office of President in the following terms: "There shall be a President . . . who shall take precedence over all persons within the State." Quite properly, in view of the status of His Irish Majesty Edward VIII, this merely invests the President with the rank of *primus inter pares*—it does not, and could not affect, or derogate from, the Royal position *vis à vis* Irish subjects of the Crown.

The Republic of Ireland Act, 1948, which came into operation on April 18 1949, repealed the Executive Authority (External Relations) Act, 1936, and provided, by section 3, that "the President, on the authority and on the advice of the Government, may exercise the executive power or any executive function of the State in or in connection with its external relations." It made no provision regarding the succession to the Throne or to the "king" for the purposes of the 1936 Act, nor, curiously, did it purport to repeal the "law of Saorstat Eireann" (the Irish Free State) referred to in section 3, subsection 2 of the 1936 Act as regulating the succession.

Section 2 of the Republic of Ireland Act declared: "The description of the State shall be the Republic of Ireland." This statement is not a declaration of a Republic, any more than the statement "The description of A.B. shall be gentleman" makes A.B. a gentleman. A great deal more is needed to confer or alter status in either case. To alter the status of Ireland a constitutional amendment would have been required; this could only be effected by a referendum (Article 46 of the Constitution).

By that Act, then, whatever may or may not have been intended, nothing in fact was altered in regard to the question of Edward VIII's kingship. The Republic Act substituted the President in place of the King for the carrying out of the "purposes" theretofore provided for by the Executive Authorities Act, leaving the other position precisely as before.

One or two further remarks may properly be added. First of all, it was suggested in the Dail debates December 11/12 1936 (a) that the Acts of Settlement and Succession were only attracted into the corpus of Irish law by Article 73 of the Constitution of 1922 in so far as their provisions did not offend Article 8° of the 1922 Constitution guaranteeing religious equality, or alternatively (b) that they were in toto attracted into that corpus by the Article of the Constitution. Both propositions are clearly wrong.

The recognition of the King in the 1921 Treaty, to which the Constitution had to conform, as the common link between the United Kingdom and the Dominions necessarily implies that the validity of these Acts was also recognised and acquiesced in. There is no difficulty in this, and if the Constitution did not so recognize them in their entirety (for they are patently not severable) then, to the extent of non-recognition, the Constitution would be ultra vires the Treaty, upon which its validity in terms depended. The truth is that they are fundamental laws, as it were standing outside and governing the Irish domestic law in the same way as the Treaty itself, in which the concept of a common kingship is basic. Indeed, one has only to state the proposition that it was ever competent in an Irish Parliament unilaterally to purport to alter the law of succession to the Throne to demonstrate its absurdity.

The Official Record of the Debates makes entertaining, if not instructive, reading. It cannot, of course, be called in aid to assist in the construction of the relevant enactments. It is nonetheless worthy of comment that, amidst the universal confusion as to the consequences of the steps then under discussion, there does at least emerge from the remarks of many of the speakers (amongst them some of the country's most eminent constitutional lawyers) a warning that these steps might prove ineffective to terminate the reign of King Edward VIII. In reply, Mr. De Valera (then President of the Executive Council) was driven to admit (col. 1472) "some sort of vague title or something of that sort is probably there." One may justifiably comment that in expressing that view he was seeing the light as through a glass darkly.

It remains also to add that in preserving the kingship of His Irish Majesty King Edward VIII, the way was prepared for the accession of his wife as Queen Consort. As a citizen of the United States it is entirely appropriate that the lady should occupy the Irish Throne, personifying as she does the close association which has always existed between monarchical Ireland and that great republic.

# Epilogue

As a result of the constitutional complexities of December 1936, whereby Edward VIII never abdicated from the Irish Free State throne, the accession of George VI did not affect his brother's kingship of that part of the British Dominions. The imbroglio was accordingly created which left Edward still King of the Irish Free State and George King-Emperor of the rest of the British Commonwealth. As Edward outlived George this absurd situation obtained until Edward's death, whereupon Elizabeth II, his niece, who had already succeeded her father to the British throne in her capacity as heir to her uncle Edward VIII, now also succeeded to that of the former Irish Free State or, if one prefers, Republic, thereby at last uniting the two Crowns, resolving one anomaly and establishing a constitutional dilemma, which is the present position.

One wonders if all this is not entirely consistent with the known legalistic proclivities of de Valera. At all times he maintained the need for "external association" with Westminster. This was a concept so vague and so symptomatic of a personality informed by a unique amalgam of Latin deviousness with peasant cunning as to accommodate pretty well any expedient constitutional circumstances might dictate. Time and again was this adroitness manifest during the war when in virtuoso displays of political high-wire acrobatics, de Valera maintained a benevolent so-called neutrality towards Britain while, at the same time, keeping the rapacity of Germany at bay when Hitler's star was at its apogee during the first three terrible years.

The general misapprehension of the side effects of the events of December 1936 is deplorable or amusing, depending upon one's point of view. Shortly after the occurrence the present Constitution was enacted, and it prohibited *inter alia* the conferring of titles of nobility. Now, while this provision may not have caused its author, de Valera, any great heart-searching, the same is clearly not so of his successors in power.

As has been pointed out in Chapter Ten, the Irish adherence to the notion of kingship, which, of course, implies the existence of an aristocracy, would appear to be completely inhibited by the annoying prohibition of the legal constraints of the Constitution. Given the inveterate snobbishness of the Gael, and particularly of the present variety thereof, this Constitutional abscess clearly calls for lancing. The necessity for such surgery became clearer during the Irish presidency of the EEC; it mattered not at all that it rotates every six months in alphabetical order. All the stops were pulled out and joy was unconfined among the celebrants of this non-office. Instead of the more conventional reward of chicken and ham supper in the parish hall, the faithful were now invited to grace functions in the august surroundings of Dublin Castle, and the Royal Hospital.

One thing only was missing from the protocol attending these glittering scenes—the absence of a native aristocracy, and already there are murmurs from on high which one prays do not forebode an Irish supplement to the *Almanach de Gotha*. Be that as it may, it was mischievously discovered that there was no restraint upon the award of academic as distinct from social distinction. The result was of course foreseeable, and for the old jibe at Dublin being the "City of Dreadful Knights", is now substituted that of "Dubious Doctors": unfortunately the infection is now endemic, and has so spread nationwide that a new class of doctorate has now been created as a kind of social service for the educationally deprived.

Strange are the uses of constitutional law!

When one turns from a contemplation of the sailing to the windward of the fundamental law of the land by emperors with no clothes, and doctors with no learning, to a consideration of the estimation in which the profession charged with the administration of that law is held by the politicians, the outlook is less than auspicious.

Part of Ireland achieved Dominion status by virtue of the Treaty, and the consequent Constitution of 1922. At no time did the Irish people enjoy the full benefits of that Constitution, as their full domestic rights were abrogated by a series of continuous Constitutional Amendment Acts up to the coming into force of the present Constitution. On the outbreak of the Second World War, even more draconic measures were adopted, notably the Emergency Power Acts, but above all the Offences Against the State Act, 1939, which latter is still in force and drastically invades the liberty of the citizen. It is not unfair, therefore, to say that the State since its foundation has been, with a brief hiatus, in a continuous state of emergency.

This state of affairs necessarily entails that the Bar, traditionally the bulwark of the rights of the people, should be the *bête noire* of the politicians, and particularly such whose pretensions outrun their discretion: one feels impelled to deplore that there is not inculated into every member in Leinster House the apophthegm that the best politician is he who does least harm.

For the purpose of this epilogue, it is sufficient to say that, largely as a result of political pressure, the Irish Bar is in the course of an inexorable decline from a profession to a trade. The abolition of juries, for example, has done nothing to arrest the decline of oratory, although it must be said that elegance of speech in Court, even since the first edition of this book, is now rare indeed.

This deterioration, however, one fears is only symptomatic of a debasement of standards generally at the Bar. One looks back nostalgically to times when the camaraderie of the Bar was a reality, and which the radical upheaval in the code of conduct for, and constitution of, the Bar of Ireland presaged at its general meeting does nothing to re-establish.

The necessity for certain reforms was recognised by the Bar itself, not least, one feels, in regard to the absurdly inflated influx into the profession. This has roughly quadrupled since this book was written, and the fact that a very sizeable percentage consists of people who never intended to practise Law, has produced a situation where traditions are either unknown or ignored. These are too often replaced by those of the market place which produces so many budding barristers who come into the somewhat benignly termed category of "mature" students. This maturity embraces persons of advancing years who, having reached retirement age, prefer the amenities of the Law Library to reliving their commercial or bureaucratic triumphs with their senescent contemporaries.

This situation, while it cannot be laid at the door of the Minister for Industry and Commerce, must however gladden his heart. It is noteworthy that while the Minister for Justice, in whose province one would have thought the affairs of the Bar would be paramount, is all in all well disposed, the enmity of his colleague would appear to be inveterate, and every possible opportunity to subvert the Irish Bar is availed of by him. The qualifications of this Minister to maintain his attack stem from his connection with the Fair Trade Commission, whose report is in many respects a model of ineptitude. They can hardly be based upon his incumbency of a ministry which comprehends responsibility for an industrial and commercial area infected with the highest per capita unemployment rate in Europe.

On that discordant note it is perhaps time in this postscript to turn to a few recollections evocative of the last twenty-five years.

Unquestionably, the outstanding judge was Cearbhall Ó Dálaigh, who played such unexpected tunes upon the constitutional instrument supplied to him by de Valera as not even that ingenious gentleman could have anticipated. In doing so, Ó Dálaigh, together with his admirable colleague and juristic successor, Brian Walsh, created a corpus of constitutional jurisprudence which will remain a perennial model. It is a not unfitting reflection upon our politicians that in the course of their squalid transactions such a man should have been forced from public life.

Another indelible impact, for very different reasons, upon both litigants and practitioners was made by a judge who has since departed to his reward, if that is the appropriate expression. While the target of this gentleman's animosity was usually the plaintiff, his splenetic ingenuity was such as to distribute impartial dissatisfaction, combined with a sense of injustice, to everyone associated with litigation in his court, and not least the witness. A spectacular instance of this resourcefulness was supplied on an occasion when he sat as a Judge of Assize. In a triangular action, all three parties and their legal teams were observed outside the courthouse crying out to heaven for vengeance, as a result of His Lordship's decision, against which there was no appeal; and by no means mute was a witness who had journeyed from Dublin formally to prove a document, and was characterised as a perjurer for his pains.

Similar judicial *tours-de-force* achieved a climax in Green Street when the Judge informed defending counsel that he was "a disgrace to the Irish Bar".

The object of this blandishment paused for insolent reflection before observing, "May I venture to suggest that there could, perhaps, be more than one view about that; I can, however, assure your Lordship that there are no two views about you"!

As if to reinforce this assessment, the rape of the King's Inns Library will always remain as a monument to his memory. The dispersal from what was one of the great collections in these islands, of priceless books and manuscripts, for whatever meretricious reason, remains one of breathtaking vandalism. If such a cultural outrage were committed in war-time, while it might not rank in enormity with the destruction of the Library of Louvain by the Germans in 1914, or of Monte Cassino by the Allies in 1945, it would be none the less criminal.

Truly, Peace has its atrocities no less than War!

All, however, has not changed.

A visitor from any other country with a legal system when contemplating our statute law, and Constitution, would indeed be surprised to learn that the Irish language is not that used in the everyday life of the Irish people. Were he informed that very few cases indeed in the Superior Courts are conducted in Irish, his surprise would, no doubt, turn to incredulity, and were he further informed that, despite the debates on the Constitution and its amendments being conducted in English, and that that instrument enacts that the Irish version takes precedence over the English where there is an ambiguity, his incredulity would turn to disbelief. This nonsense was embodied as a legal imperative in the Constitution by its onlie begetter, which must induce anyone with a sense of humour to the reflection that if de Valera did not exist he should have been invented. In fact he was, by Lewis Carroll when he created Humpty Dumpty, who it will be remembered informed Alice that words meant exactly what he wanted them to mean. That this principle be sanctified into a canon of legal construction is entirely characteristic of the great panjandrum.

To consider further this fascinating theme, one assumes that only the sacred cow of patriotism could first of all have suggested this linguistic status, and secondly have accorded it uncritical respect. Dr Johnson said, "Patriotism is the last refuge of a scoundrel", to which sentiment, were he a modern Irishman, he would surely have added "and a humbug". While entirely approving any movement dedicated to the preservation and resuscitation of the

Irish language, one feels that before it achieves legal precedence it should await the day when it enjoys the standing of being a vernacular of the Irish people, whose rights and duties can be crucially determined by the Supreme Court's interpretation of an article of the Constitution.

That this happy day is hardly imminent may be inferred from the unfortunate circumstance that in the dying days of British rule there were roughly three hundred thousand native Irish speakers, which figure has declined to less than ten thousand under our present dispensation.

Moreover, the unreality of the provisions which confer the accolade of first official language upon Irish can be illustrated by reference to the last referendum. For the purpose of his submissions to the Supreme Court which involved an interpretation of the text of the Bill, counsel for the applicant sought from the Government Information Services the Irish text of the proposed amendment. Although this request was made three weeks after the Bill had passed the Dáil and had been referred to the people, the Irish text, he was informed, was still in the process of preparation. The legal implication of this remarkable position is that not merely is the highest court in the land called upon to give effect to the translation of the original, but a translation which had never been before the legislature or the people, much less voted upon.

This certainly gives a new dimension to the concept of government by the Civil Service, an institution which will no doubt continue to bend its efforts to the fruitful productions of versions of the Statutes which will reach a readership roughly equivalent to that of the Dead Sea Scrolls. Despite, however, this esoteric class, the late Professor John Kelly gives several instances where the Supreme Court has, in its construction, given effect to the Irish version. One of these may suffice to illustrate the danger inherent in this procedure. In his determination as to what legally constitutes a *decision* of the Central Criminal Court, O'Higgins CJ triumphantly announced that the Irish version which, incidentally, had never been referred to up to then by either the Court or Counsel, comprehends in its interpretation a simple finding of "not guilty" by a jury. He referred to the Irish word "breith" meaning a "decision" as concluding the matter. Had this important finding been debated, it would have been pointed out that the jury system, unknown as it was to the Brehon Law, could not have been appropriate to the word "breith", apart altogether from the ineluctable infirmity in any attempt to ascertain the precise legal meaning of a word in Irish that there is no standard dictionary or other yardstick to which recourse can be had. Anyone who doubts has only to look at the perpetrations in the bilingual signs of our local authorities.

Finally, just as the old order is passing, so, of course, in the nature of things is its personnel. Such people may be characterised as barristers, with a liberal education, often in the classics, who entered the profession by the hallway rather than a trade by the back door. This is far from implying that many did not have rich and rewarding lives, before and after being called. Prominent in this category was the late, and ever to be lamented, William Hurley, who died in harness as librarian in the Law Library a year or so ago, in his nineties. As Bill himself would be the first to mock at any mawkishness, it is enough to say that his death not merely marked the passing of an era, but in the real sense of two eras.

It is almost inconceivable, but true, that as a second lieutenant in the Royal Flying Corps, Bill flew a fighter plane against the famous circus of Von Richtofen, and later, after the latter's death, and on the formation of the RAF, as a pilot officer, against his successor, Hermann Goering, who had assumed command of the squadron.

Hurley's later activities were no less notable, including as they did his being commanding officer of Aircraftsman

Shaw, better known as T.E. Lawrence of Arabia. Bill finished up as Group Captain, full of years, and honours, but was entirely unassuming. So much so that during an interview with Aer Lingus when, having applied for a temporary job during the Long Vacation which would keep him near his beloved aeroplanes, his interlocutor, who was a pretentious young upstart, enquired as to the airfields to which he (Bill) had been attached during the War.

Bill strung off a number of bases on which he had served, whereupon he was asked somewhat testily:

"What was your last posting?"

"Catterick Air Base."

"As an aircraftsman, I suppose?"

"Well—not exactly."

"As what then?"

"As a matter of fact I was in charge."

It can be confidently predicted that there shall be no more Bill Hurleys. The winds of competition which blow so balmily through the corridors of power can be trusted to dissipate the graciousness and good fellowship of a once great profession, which apprehension is well illustrated by the malicious invention by a member of the old school of a sketch based on the BBC Mastermind programme, featuring a well known personal injuries counsel as the contestant:

*Questionmaster:* "You are a Senior Counsel, and have chosen as your specialised subject "The Practice of the Law". Now for your first question: "What is a tort?"

*Contestant:* "Pass."

*Quizmaster:* "What is a contract?"

*Contestant:* "Pass."

*Questionmaster:* "What is a crime?"

*Contestant:* "Pass."

*Questionmaster:* "With how many insurance claims managers did your rival Mr. X dine last week?"

*Contestant:* "Five."

Amusing, but the lampoon is no less pungent than ominous if The Law Library, as one fears, is to be invaded by tradesmen on the make, of an ilk which inspired one of the old school to enquire when informed that a dinner in honour of one of the more gauche of his colleagues was to be given in the King's Inns:

"How interesting! Shall there be knives and forks?"

One could have assured him that whatever about the dinner table, there shall be knives in the Law Library.

REX MACKEY
10 July 1991

# Index